DANCING IN THE DARK

DANCING IN THE DARK

The crossing of Europe's highest ice-cap by an integrated team of disabled and able-bodied people

Stephen Miles Bull

MERLIN BOOKS

First published in Great Britain, 1995

Quotations from *Winnie-the-Pooh* by A. A. Milne: kind permission of Methuen Children's Books

Published by Merlin Books Ltd.
Braunton, Devon, England

British Library Cataloguing in Publication Data
A catalogue record for this book is available from the British Library

ISBN 0 86303 722–4

Printed in England by Orchard & Ind Ltd., Gloucester.

This book is dedicated to the following people,

long suffering in different ways:

All the staff and pupils at Fountaindale School;

my parents, Miles and Jennifer Bull, and Mr and Mrs L. Sedgwick;

A girl who is out there somewhere

AUTHOR'S NOTE

I would like to thank Sir Ranulph Fiennes for staking his fantastic reputation on an unknown explorer by agreeing to act as Patron. For an extremely busy man he has always responded promptly and patiently to my hastily scribbled letters.

An expedition is also only as good as its team. All my team-mates, despite a lack of experience, were magnificent in almost every aspect.

During the final writing of this book my grandfather, Frank Bull, died, blind for many years he never once complained.

CONTENTS

Front cover photograph: Steve Bull and Zelda Garner on the Jostedalsbreen ice-cap
Back cover photograph: Mick Barnes manhauling

It's an expedition.

That's what an expedition means. A long line of everybody.

You'd better tell the others to get ready.

A. A. Milne, 1926

ACKNOWLEDGEMENTS

Without the help of all of the following, the expedition would never have got as far as Newcastle, never mind Norway. If it wasn't for the support of local business and industry no expedition would ever go anywhere.

I am deeply grateful to all.

BCB International Ltd. Cardiff
Cowen & Partners, Mansfield
Monitor Coatings, Tyne & Wear
The Princes Trust
Broughton Brothers
The Plungar Village Committee, Plungar
Air Training Corps Association, 384 Sqn
The British Paralympic Association
South Midlands Communications, Eastliegh
Mark Shearer
Sir Ranulph Fiennes
Bullwell Precision Engineers, Pinxton
Fountaindale School, Mansfield
The Royal Geographical Society
Ted Grey
Tesco, Mansfield
Safeway, Mansfield
Mr & Mrs W. M. Bull
Hall Textiles, Mansfield
Bill Blackamore, Notts. Youth & Community
Kodak Ltd.
DeMontford University
Natwest Bank, Mansfield
The Sherwood Foresters Association
Neil Ritson, BP, Norway
Positioning Resources, Aberdeen
Kirkby Rotary Club
Notts. County Council
Wellington College
D. J. Mordaunt
Rochelle Broxap
Susan Dawson
Mr & Mrs L. Sedgwick
Dukeries School, Ollerton
Paul Barrow
Ann Leyland
The Paul Vander Molen Foundation
Geoff Jones
Sally Emslie
Susan Howard
Iceland Frozen Foods PLC

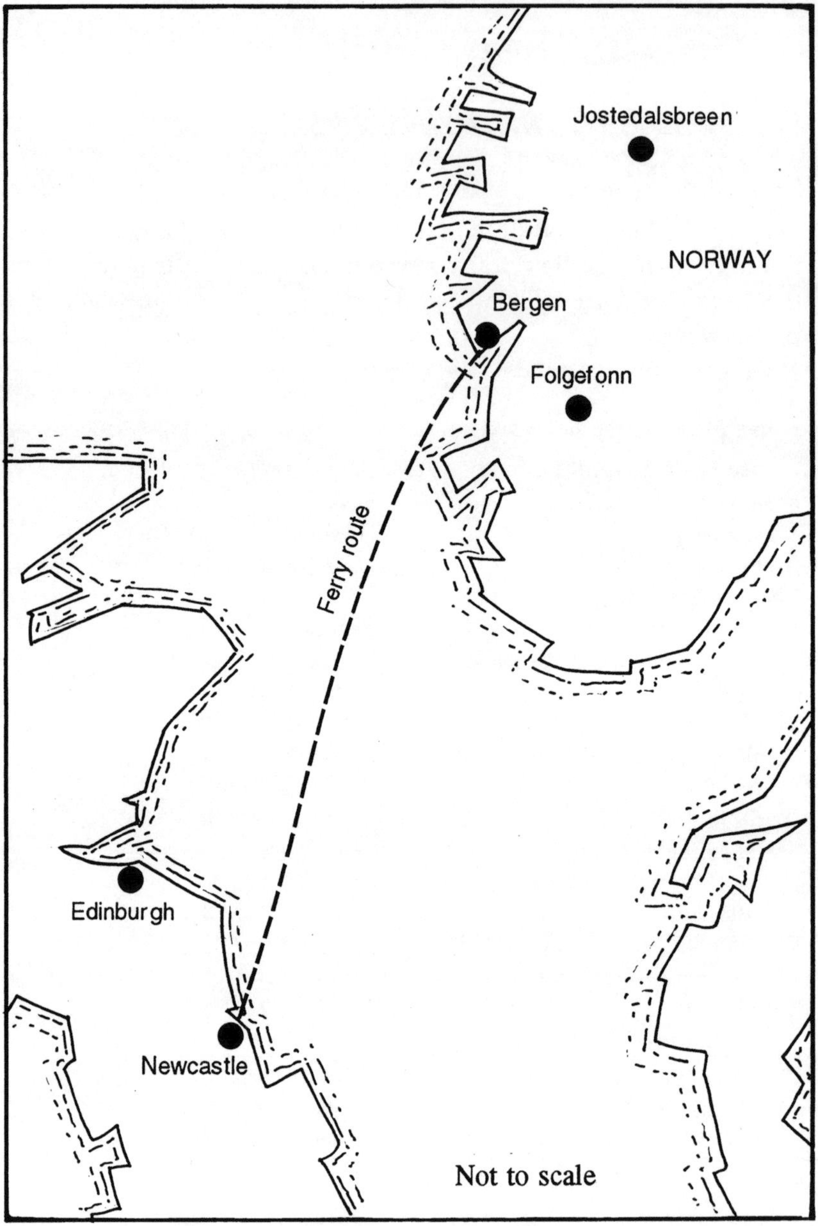

Map showing the position of Jostedalsbreen and Folgefonn

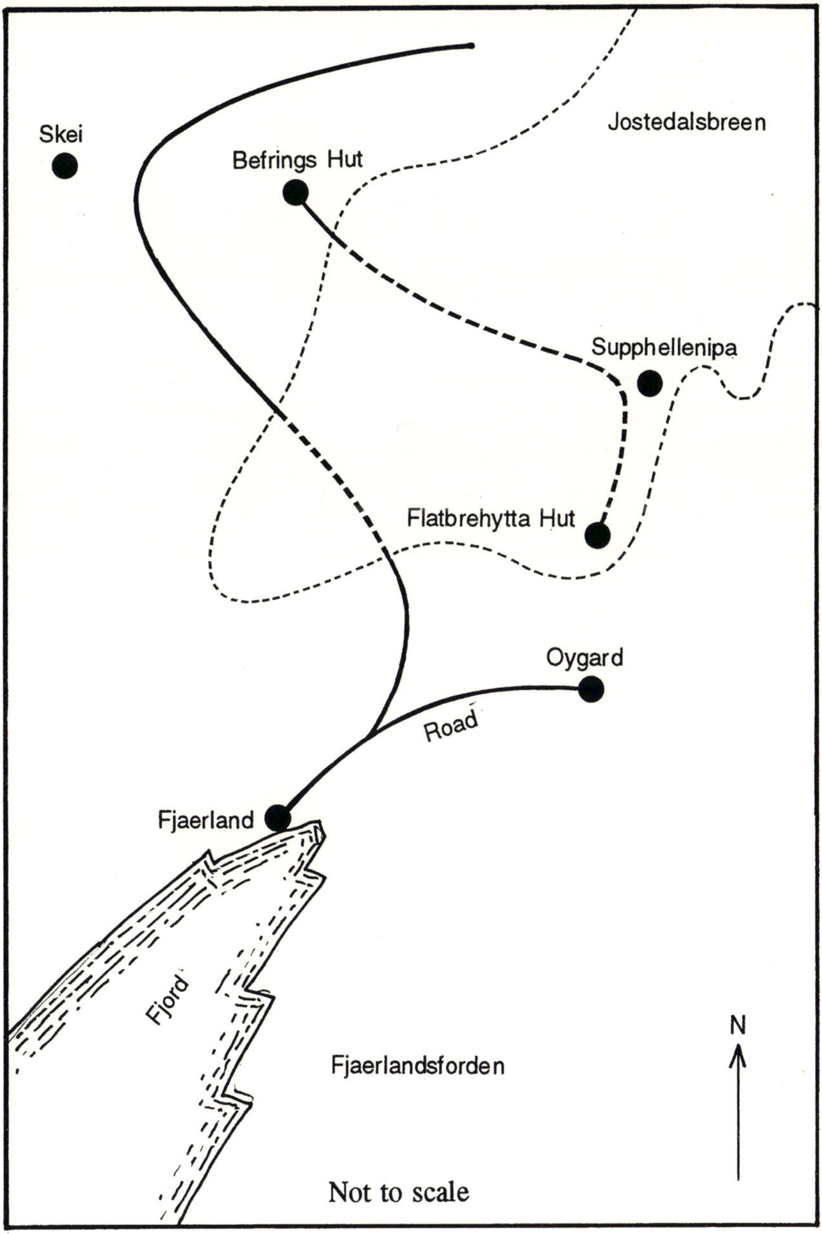

Map showing the route taken across Jostedalsbreen

FOREWORD

Crossing ice-caps and travelling over glaciers is a dangerous activity at the best of times. To do so if one is visually impaired is doubly courageous. I offer my congratulations to all members of Steve Bull's team for completing a physically demanding task in hostile terrain. They tackled a number of serious obstacles in a most impressive way. The experience was obviously rewarding for them all.

Through involvement with both the Paul Vander Molen Foundation and the Calvert Trust I have the greatest admiration for disabled people who tackle the great outdoors.

Having been to Jostedalsbreen in the 1960s I appreciate the challenges Steve's team faced and offer my congratulations to all the team members.

This book describes the crossing of Europe's highest ice-cap by a team of able-bodied and disabled people working together to realize a difficult but worthwhile dream.

Sir Ranulph Fiennes

INTRODUCTION

You've got to be your own hero, find it out for yourself.
Bruce Springsteen

If the medical profession is correct in its diagnosis about my knees, in three or four years' time I will be confined to a wheelchair. When and if this is the case I will look back to the summer of 1994 with a certain nostalgia. For that was the time I strode down the Flatbrehytta glacier on Europe's highest ice-cap, the Jostedalsbreen ice-cap in central Norway.

I well remember the cold evening wind in my face, the fluttering of a flag and the only sound that of my sledge as it glided across the snow.

Yet the doctors may be wrong and Norway may be the stepping-stone to bigger and better things.

In the late twentieth century there are very few last great challenges left. If your interest is in the realms of ice and snow then there are even fewer. I can think of probably only two 'last great polar challenges'. As a result, those of us with a restless spirit need to look further afield to quench a desire which 100 years ago would have earned fame and fortune.

There is a group of people in our society, though, for whom the march of geographical mastery is not of the same rate. Disabled people have so far participated little in the field of private expeditions. This is not, I'm sure, due to lack of interest on their part. It is simply because the opportunity has not presented itself. Many people may have heard of Norman Croucher or John Hawkridge, both men with severe disabilities who have ventured out into the hills. Yet these men are probably an exception to a false rule.

This book is about the Integrated Norway Expedition which included disabled people in its framework as equals. Probably this is nothing new, but personally I've never come across an expedition book covering the same topic. It would have been useful to read one whilst planning the expedition! Hopefully, this should provide an initial guide on how to plan and execute an expedition involving disabled people. Also, when I was putting the expedition together I set out to read as much as I could about the Jostedalsbreen ice-cap. Apart from a few guide books which are about, there are hardly any travel books on the area. About time to put the deficit straight, I thought!

Finally, my last reason for attempting to write a book is that I have no money, no reputation and little experience. When I read a travel book I always wonder how the explorer in question got started in expeditions. How did they raise the money? How was the team selected? This book aims to tell this side of the story, how it is possible to have a dream and make it come true.

This may not be a tale of epic endurance, of surviving against the odds, however, it is about the magic and romance of ice-cap travel, the integration of disabled people into expeditions and a *Boys' Own*, old-fashioned adventure.

Sometimes an expedition book stands or falls on its colour photographs. In this book, though, I have used only stark, dramatic black and white prints because it was the haunting black and white photos of Scott and his men which inspired me. Old polar expedition photos to me are magical, a timeless record of hardship and glory. Maybe one of the photos in this book will inspire someone to venture out into the wilderness, preferably with an integrated team.

1

LEGENDARY INSPIRATION

I hear the echoes through the mountains throng,
The winds come to me from the fields of sleep.
Wordsworth

My first can of beer tasted fantastic. I can clearly remember sitting in the back of an old Escort estate completely exhausted after having walked thirty-four miles along what is known as the White Rose Walk. When I went to school the following day the headmaster was most interested to learn why a nine-year-old under his charge should undertake such a venture. My answer was simple, 'I went for a walk with my dad.' Some walk!

Two years later I stared at the black and white photograph of five tired men. Even then the faces of Scott and his party evoked disturbing ambitions inside me. On my White Rose Walk I had experienced something akin to hardship and discomfort. (Or so I thought at the impressionable age of eleven.) If you look closely at the photograph of Scott it is not hard to imagine what they all went through. In some timeless way they speak out, a tale of adventure, of heroes and ultimately tragedy.

Time marched on for me though; school came and went, followed by a short and uneventful career in the Royal Air Force. More by luck than design I found myself in Chichester undergoing the first year of a degree course. Bored of academic study into the sociology of sport, I picked up a book from a shop shelf. *In The Footsteps of Scott* it read. I read on; it grabbed me by the short and curlies, so to speak, and I didn't read a book on sport for two days.

It had seemed an age since I had last read about Antarctica; here was the motivation to sustain me through three years of study. I resolved to go on an expedition. It didn't matter where, anywhere would do. Romantic visions of yomping into the unknown filled my head; I read everything I could on the Antarctic and the Arctic. Rather than the names of eminent sports physiologists filling my head I had names like Shackleton, Watkins and Mawson cramming my mind.

With such enthusiasm it is not hard to get on an expedition. Unfortunately Antarctic expeditions are still rare but ones to Africa aren't. Before I knew it I'd accepted a place to go on an organized expedition to Africa at the end of my degree course. It wasn't quite the far south but it was a start. Although I couldn't yet go to the polar regions I could still read about them. By twisting the rules somewhat I managed to convince the college that they should let me do my dissertation on polar exploration, which once undertaken led me to a meeting that changed the next few years of my life.

John Wright explored the polar wastes of Iceland, Spitsbergen and Ellesmere Island during the late 1930s. When I met him at his home in west Sussex he still had the same zest for life that must have carried him across the frozen lands of the north. We talked for two hours on all aspects of polar exploration. After having only read about such exploits, here was a man who had actually done them. He inspired me and humoured me and tempered my schoolboy ambitions with realism. When I left, he suggest I go and visit the Scott Polar Research Institute at Cambridge. 'They'll watch you and see what you're like,' he said, 'just like I've done this morning.' As he said this a big grin spread across his face. John Wright suggested that rather than go on an organized trip, it would be far more useful for me to go on my own trip. It didn't matter about the size or scale of the expedition, it was the doing that counted.

As I walked down the drive I thought about his words. If Iceland was good enough for Wright then it was good enough for me. All of a sudden a feeling of complete and utter satisfaction came over me, and the certainty that all would be well. Very few men have inspired me in such a way that John Wright did. Like morning dew in summertime my plans to go to Africa faded away, I rejected the offer and headed to the local Mrs Miggins. Half an hour later I sat in my favourite tea and cake shop and planned my first expedition.

For five weeks during the summer of '92 Susan Dawson and myself carried out an investigation into lichens on the edge of the Vatnajokull ice-cap, Iceland. We climbed on to the ice-cap, traversed the glaciers tumbling down from the ice and learnt what it is like to live and work in the field. A mythical land of bewitching and spellbinding beauty, Iceland was our training ground.

Only by doing can one find out what an expedition involves; we got dirty, we fought, we argued and we learnt. I think that I learnt more about leadership in those five weeks than I did in all my time in the Air Force. It provided a stepping-stone for future trips, once the memory had been forgotten.

My overriding memory of Iceland was of the ice-caps. My dreams of going south resurfaced, yet at that moment I needed more experience. I had forgotten the ninety pound rucksack load and the taste of freeze-dried food, only the snow and ice disappearing into the distance occupied my dreams.

In a local second-hand bookshop I found a book by Ranulph Fiennes on an expedition he had done to the Jostedalsbreen ice-cap in Norway. On reading more, I discovered the ice-cap was the largest in mainland Europe. Here seemed to be an excellent way to gain more experience in ice-cap travel without the cost and hassle of going all the way to Greenland or Antarctica.

An expedition to me means that you go and do something that hasn't been done before; too often many trips become glorified holidays. I resolved to take an expedition to Jostedalsbreen in order to do something that had never been done before.

At the time I was half-way through a teacher training course. For some reason I had signed up to train to be a PE teacher. From the very start I regretted it, that is until I found myself at a school which caters for physically handicapped children. Children who have no life as we know it, lived life to the full and appreciated everything you did for them. This was in stark contrast to the 'normal' secondary schools where we did most of our training.

Looking back now I cannot remember the initial idea; it is lost in the mists of time, in a year of incredible personal heartache and change. Before I knew it a brochure was sent out proclaiming that the aim of the Integrated Norway Expedition was to cross the highest ice-cap in Europe with a disabled team. It was then in the January of 1993. I aimed to carry out the trip the same summer.

At about the same time I went to see a man by the name of Andrew Croft. I had already met him the previous year before I went to Iceland. He is of the same stock as John Wright and has held the Guinness world record for the longest unsupported sledge journey. We met at his London home to talk about what we did in Iceland. As with John Wright I was inspired and humbled by what this man had done. The talk centred around Iceland, Captain Scott, exploration and expeditions in general. Here was a man who knew many members of Scott's fateful expedition, who had been to see Shackleton lecture, and more recently been an adviser to Ran Fiennes on his Transglobe expedition. If I couldn't learn anything from Andrew Croft then I would never learn anything about exploration.

Andrew Croft went to Greenland in an age when exploration meant exploring. In the present day we use the term 'explorer' yet no one really explores any more, at least not in the truest sense of the word. Even Peary had the foresight to realize he was born in a time when he could be an explorer: 'I am glad that my lot is cast upon the world now rather than later when there will be no new places.'

In the late twentieth century the new places are hard to find; explorers have sought out different ways of achieving the same goal. Our Norway expedition aimed to provide a new place to people who would never get the chance to explore. In my own mind this qualifies as exploration. I believe that 'exploring' is attempting something new, something that has never been tried before. We all undergo personal exploration to some extent, yet this is somewhat different to the classical meaning. To my mind 'classical' exploring is coming up with an original idea and seeing it through to the bitter end. It should involve some degree of physical and emotional hardship, an expedition first of some extent, forged friendships and bitter arguments, helping society and finally of course, planting the Union Flag for Queen and country.

2

THE ROLLING STONE

When nose of camel get through tent door rest soon follow.
Anon

It was one thing to talk about expeditions, to dream of going on them, quite another prospect to carry one out. Iceland had been no real problem because one sponsor had backed us, also only two of us went. The practicalities of getting it off the ground only took six months.

A combination of blind optimism and ignorance made me think I could organize the Norway project in the same time span whilst training to be a teacher.

I aimed to go in July. In the space of six months I needed a team of twelve people, two vehicles, and enough equipment and money to spend three weeks in Norway. So many people have said to me since we came back from Norway, 'I wouldn't know where to start.' In reality, as soon as the first move is made then it is easier to carry on than back out, or so I found anyway!

I'm sure everyone organizes a trip in different ways. My first priority was to sort out a letterhead and brochure. Once this is done it is just a matter of sending it off to likely sponsors. Of course it isn't as simple as this in reality but somehow it seems to work for me, just.

Rather than doing loads of fund-raising events, the aim was to target certain companies for either cash donations or donations in kind. When approaching companies it is vital that they know exactly what you are doing and how much you want from them and for what. We needed to have an exact plan and aim so we could convince people to part with their money.

One evening in March I received a phone call from a chap called Mick Coyne. I recognized the name as being that of a representative of the Paul Vander Molen Foundation. 'Excellent!' I thought, he must be phoning me up to offer some money. Being an organization which caters specifically for helping trips such as ours, I felt that we needed their support.

'Hallo, is that Steve Bull?'

'Yes, speaking.'

'Mick Coyne here. You are going to Norway aren't you? Only I've got this letter from you and the only bit I can read is the letterhead. I reckon you could do with some advice on writing letters.'

This was a major blow to my fund-raising strategy. If Mick couldn't read my writing then no one else could. This probably explained why I had received very few replies so far.

Over the phone I set out to explain what we aimed to do in Norway during the coming summer.

On the face of it the plan was simple. Jostedalsbreen ice-cap has been crossed hundreds of times, yet, as far as I could ascertain, not by a disabled team and certainly not by someone confined to a wheelchair. I explained to Mick that we would travel to Norway by ferry. Once in Bergen we would drive north to the ice-cap. Once there we would attempt to cross the ice-cap along its spine, a distance of some eighty miles. In terms of a purely able-bodied expedition, such a crossing is nothing unusual. However, I soon realized as people questioned how we were going to do this, that such a task was not a simple one.

Actually crossing the ice-cap presented no real problem as we would tow equipment on sledges. Our wheelchair-user would propel himself by means of an adapted downhill sit ski. We also aimed to include a visually-impaired person in the team which would increase the credibility of our integration philosophy. The integration of disabled people into the expedition was our crux philosophy. Rather than purely providing a pedestal for them, I expected all our disabled members to work alongside their able-bodied counterparts as much as possible. Rather than gearing the expedition to their needs they had to fit into the project's framework. Only by doing this would it be a truly integrated expedition. In the practical terms this meant that they would be asked to help with the cooking, cleaning and look after themselves as much as possible. It was these chores that were to create much tension when we actually put the philosophy into action and provide a few quite emotional moments.

At about this time, as the first batch of brochures arrived at local companies and I delivered lectures on Iceland where I mentioned the Norway project, people questioned the rationale in taking disabled people. Could it be true that you are taking disabled people in order to further your own ambition? Such a comment came up more than once, and as a result I feel this is as good a place as any to define my rationale.

I make no bones about the fact that I am ambitious to pursue a career in the field of expeditions. Yet I also feel a need to help people. If I had an academic learning I would like to pursue a medical career. However, I have decidedly more brawn than grey matter. Taking a disabled person on an expedition would serve both my ambitions. In the present financial climate one has to be something of a mercenary in order to put together an expedition, certainly a private one. Finance rules to a certain extent what you can achieve and who you will take. Such a situation virtually doomed the expedition once in the field, as a result of selecting team members on whether they could pay the fees set, even though the cost per expedition member was very low in comparison to other trips.

The idea of walking across an ice-cap didn't appeal to most of my close friends. Sue gave the idea some thought, yet the memory of Iceland was a little too fresh. By word of mouth people became interested. My only criteria for selecting team members was that they should be keen, committed and have £300. If everyone who had applied for the trip actually came then we would have been over fifteen strong.

As I planned to go in six months, things were organized on a wing and a prayer. No one was really committed and money was sparse in coming in. At one stage we had two Land Rovers and ten people. With a week to go we lost the Land Rovers and the money to pay for the ferry, I split up with my girlfriend and the external examiner came down to assess my teaching. It was all going horribly wrong. The dream which had begun in the cold of winter was melting away in the heat of summer. No training had been done and we hadn't even all met.

A decision needed to be made and quickly. There was no way I was going to give in, although everyone said at the time that was the best thing to do. Fate dealt a hand. It was a double-edged sword that saved the expedition yet broke my heart. I was in Sheffield staying with a friend who supported the expedition. In complete contrast, I visited my girlfriend who had backed me a great deal regarding the venture. She had recently terminated our relationship believing it was for the best. As usual I was too stubborn to agree with her. I had been a rat to her but couldn't see it. We talked for the last time and I walked into the Peaks. With nowhere to go I went back to Julian's house. He saw straight away that I needed cheering up. Boddington's beer is a good counsellor, yet he aimed to introduce me to a friend of his who shared the same interest in expeditions. The introduction was to be the turning point. As I look back now on that weekend, it seems to me that if I hadn't seen my girlfriend I would never have met Mark Shearer. Only by becoming obsessed in Norway could I forget the girl I will always love.

From the start Mark was keen on the expedition. We decided to postpone it till the following year. In the meantime we would put on an expedition to Norway to assess the feasibility of taking disabled people on to the ice-cap. As soon as the decision was taken to postpone it, the expedition began to happen. Our sponsors agreed to the idea along with the team members. I now had another year to put right the mistakes I had made so far. The nose of the camel had been led through the tent door; according to the proverb, the rest would soon follow. What I hadn't realized at the time was that getting the nose through was the easy part. Getting the humps through was to be a different prospect altogether.

Since Ranulph Fiennes had been to the same ice-cap we intended going to, I figured he might be someone to approach for patronage. I had written to him before his Antarctic crossing with reference to my dissertation. Ran Fiennes receives hundreds of letters from budding explorers so it was with some surprise a letter arrived indicating he would be happy to be our patron. In contrast to Fiennes's popularity, a friend of mine once approached Charlie Burton about an expedition of his to Iceland. Charlie Burton was so astounded by such a request he agreed straight away. No one had ever approached him before even though he had stood at both the South and North Poles along with Fiennes on the epic Transglobe trip.

With the patronage of an eminent explorer behind us Mark Shearer and I set off for central Norway to carry out the reconnaissance expedition. At this stage we still aimed to take a wheelchair-bound person up on to and across the ice-cap. Ignorance and boldness are useful qualities needed to start an expedition; they become redundant once the project is up and running. I needed now to exchange my ignorance for knowledge and temper my boldness with caution. It was the September of 1993. The Norwegian summer was coming to an end. Winter was looming over the horizon and with it a crucial stage in the expedition.

3

LAND OF DREAMS

Lo, would I flee far away, and live in the wilderness.
Psalm 55

Extending over 486 square kilometres, Jostedalsbreen is by far the largest area of ice and snow on the continent of Europe. It has been crossed and climbed extensively by all nationalities. However, our purpose was to see if we could get a wheelchair with someone in it on to it, something that has definitely not been done before. Could it be done?

Depending on the weather you either experience a one-disco crossing or two-disco crossing. Compliments of Colour line ferries, Mark and I experienced the ship's band twice. Spending longer on the ferry than planned did have its compensation though. The journey enabled both of us to get to know one another. There are many ways to see if someone is suited to expedition work, some more demanding than others. I've found that if you can get on well with someone over the customary few beers then that is as good a rule of thumb as any.

Mark had the experience to temper my enthusiasm. Having climbed in the Himalayas and the north face of the Eiger he was the perfect choice for the conditions we were likely to encounter. Being also a qualified nurse was a bonus.

Due to financial restrictions we were travelling light. Even so I was relieved to hand my rucksack into the care of the bus driver who was to drive us north. North at last. Norway is much like Scotland, yet bigger. Much bigger. As we drove north we stared out at mountains which rose straight out of the sea. It is easy to make comparisons with the Alps. True, the Alps are higher, but you don't see them blasting straight out of the water; sheer walls of rock reaching for the sky.

In time we came to the Sognefjord. The fjord that links the sea to the southern aspect of the ice-cap is also breathtaking. As we boarded the ferry which would take us to Fjaerland our eyes strained for a glimpse of the ice-cap. Two hours and two cheeseburgers later the ice rose out of the fjord ahead. The sky was bright blue, the snow like icing, all reflected in the deep dark waters.

The land of dreams had become a reality. We departed the ferry, opened a can of beer and contemplated our good fortune. It was late in the afternoon. After what seemed for ever it was decided that before dark, we'd make it up to the Flatbrehytta glacier and a small hut we had found on the map. Bad move. In our haste and high spirits we'd only glanced at the map without paying great attention to the scale. It didn't look very far on the map, did it?

Over fifty years ago Eric Oygard's father (the local farmer) built the Flatbrehytta hut on the edge of the ice-cap. The original hut still stands along with a newer addition added in recent years. Together they look out over one of the most splendid views in central Norway.

Over 1,000 metres below two young men stood in the early evening light confidently predicting it wouldn't be too long before they were at the hut.

Three hours later as dusk closed in we looked at the map. No amount of looking at the map could free us from the fact that we had seriously underestimated the walk up to the hut. It didn't help that we'd only eaten two cheeseburgers all day. The path was steep, narrow and rocky. It was going to be interesting getting a wheelchair up. Finally, as it got dark we saw the outline of the hut. A gift from the gods, it rose out of the gloom to greet us with open log fires, food and warmth. Boddington's beer was in order. I had one can left.

My crampons must have also been thirsty as they had punctured the can of beer soaking the majority of my kit. At least it wasn't a can of ski wax! Even this small mishap couldn't dampen our spirits, such was the splendour of our surroundings.

We had a job of work to accomplish. In order to make the main expedition a reality the next year it was vital that a safe and simple route up and on to the ice-cap was found. It was clear from our ascent that it may take several days to get a wheelchair-bound person up to the hut. The only possible way was by stretcher. Once on the ice we planned to adapt a downhill sit ski so the person in question could be self-propelled.

In the morning we had our first glimpse of the ice close up. Above us the Flatbrehytta glacier stretched away into the distance. To the side it tumbled down into the valley. All around us snowcapped mountains scraped the heavens.

Due to the exertions of the day before we spent the day exploring the immediate locality and sorting out our equipment. It felt good to be alive. In order to get an overall view of the route on to the ice-cap we planned to climb the peaks that flanked the Flatbrehytta glacier, hoping it would be possible to see the whole route up on to the upper ice-fields.

After a relaxing day an early start was made and the two of us followed the moraine on to the lower aspects of the glacier.

The feeling of being alone in the mountains is hard to beat. One couldn't have asked for better weather. Luckily most of the crevasses seemed visible and there seemed little need to rope up as we crossed the glacier. Taking our time, we picked our way between various-sized holes in the ice. There was no rush as the sun shone down and the snow was crisp and hard under our feet.

Supphellenipa rises to 1,731 metres above its namesake, the Supphellenipa glacier. From the summit it is possible to see the whole extent of the ice-cap stretching into the distance. The top of the glacier provides the gateway to Jostedalsbreen. In many ways it is similar to the Beardmore in Antarctica. Or so it seemed to an impressionable young man standing above the glacier in the clear afternoon light.

We hadn't seen a soul all day. After crossing the glacier in the morning we had climbed on to a long ridge that led to the summit of Supphellenipa. From such a viewpoint it was clear that once on the glacier there would be no real problems in getting a wheelchair-bound person on to the actual ice-cap. After taking pictures of the whole route up it was time to descend. There shouldn't be any crevasses on the way down, should there?

The route down looked simple enough. It turned out to be something of a nightmare. As always, the descent was more dangerous than the ascent. There is elation after reaching the summit. Unfortunately for us this was accompanied by relaxation.

For some reason I stopped some two feet short of a small crack in the snow. On a closer yet cautious inspection the crack widened to form the mother of all holes in the ice. Two-man glacier travel is a risky business as there is the danger that if one person falls in a crevasse the other will not be able to help.

'Who's going first?' Mark enquired.

'You should go first, you're a lot lighter than me,' I replied. It seemed logical to me that the lighter of us should venture out and pick a safe route, for obvious reasons.

'Bad idea. You're heavier, so we'll know for sure if it's safe if you go first. Trust me.' Mark evidently thought differently. So, off we set. Right from the start it was clear we were bang in the middle of a major crevasse system.

Rather like a river flows down a rocky stream bed, so does a glacier. Instead of stopper waves, there are crevasses. When the ice flows over obstructions, the pressure forms in the ice creating crevasses.

For what seemed like an age we picked a safe route through an area of extreme instability. However, it did form a bond between the pair of us. We moved quickly and efficiently. By the time we reached an area of safety and descended to the hut it was clear that both of us got on as well in the mountains as we did in the pub.

Once back in the hut we took stock of the information gained from our first foray into the mountains. There was no doubt to both of us that getting up to the hut was going to be the crux. Once on to the ice one could follow a relatively safe route up one side of the glacier. Once on to the ice-cap it should be quite straightforward. Just to check, the following day we would climb the mountains on the other side of the glacier. This would enable us to gain another perspective on the route.

That evening in the hut I read a book by Peter Lennon focusing on mountaineering in Norway. It was to be sobering reading. The fire roared away, our bellies were full and the stars shone like pinholes in the curtain of night outside. Perfect.

According to Lennon, 'considerable Nordic mountain ski-touring experience' was needed. 'In this exposed mountain situation good weather is important, almost essential,' Lennon expanded. I put the book down. It suddenly seemed to me that bringing someone who was blind, and another confined to a chair into this environment was pretty reckless at best. Looking back on the day, we had been pushed to look after just ourselves. How would we cope the next year?

I remember a saying our patron had mentioned in his book *Mind Over Matter*, 'Best not to think about it.' It seemed appropriate. It was going to be a question of mind over matter to get a disabled team across the ice-cap. As long as the team didn't mind how we achieved the overall aim it didn't matter, did it?

In the morning of another crystal clear day our bodies sought to remind us of the previous day's exertions. We packed our sacks and headed up to the mountains which flanked the opposite side of the glacier. With luck we should be able to get a better view of the route on to the plateau. As the sun beat down, the hut receded into the distance and we gained height.

Although not of the same scale, the mountains situated around the Jostedalsbreen are very much Alpine in character. Steep snow slopes, rocky ridges and stunning backdrops form the essence of these Norwegian mountains.

After a week of exploration and consideration it was clear we could get someone in a chair up and on to the ice. It would be tough but possible. The same applied to a blind person. Unfortunately we had neither the time nor money to travel to the north-east tip of the ice-cap where we intended descending. Yet by examining the maps and talking to local guides, a suitable route was found.

Jostedalsbreen ice-cap is effectively a long spine of ice that stretches for approximately fifty miles south-west to north-east. Our expedition intended to traverse this spine, becoming flexible if the need arose.

Having achieved all our objectives Mark and I set out on the road home. However, by this stage money had become sparse. Unfortunately we could only pay the owner of the mountain hut a small amount of what we owed him. At the time we didn't think anything of it. Yet in a year's time it was to become a major problem on the expedition.

As luck would have it we met up and became friends with a Norwegian from Oslo and his girlfriend. Before we knew it the ice-cap was fast disappearing in the rear window of a Golf GTI.

Bergen is Norway's premier city on the west coast. In no time at all the snow and ice had become a memory, a cherished nugget to recall once I returned to England. As far as I was concerned England was no more the 'green and pleasant land' Blake had described.

Not only is Bergen a premier city, it also has premier prices to go with it. Our Norwegian friend was hard on the case trying to find us the cheapest place in Bergen to stay. His work was cut out. An hour later and an expensive mobile phone bill to go with it, we had secured a room in Madam Spoud's guest-house...

Madame Spoud's guest-house was the cheapest place in Bergen. Just one look and it was easy to see why. Situated in an area of Bergen dedicated to back alleys and construction plots, it occupies land providing exclusive views of an excellent building site. Indeed, Madame Spoud's was part of the building site. Our room had fantastic views of the local bar, a bar which that night was to provide live coverage of Norway v. England. Not the best place to be really, seeing that England lost and consequently failed to reach the World Cup finals. In two days' time the ferry left for Newcastle. Two days without money or food. Just another typical expedition really.

In a bid to relieve boredom we visited every free museum in Bergen. Our two days in Bergen proved to be the most testing of the trip. However, early on a Thursday morning we strode with light hearts to the ferry terminal. The journey home passed by without any great mishap. There was the usual copious amounts of beer consumed in the bar with the usual results. England's dull coast showed itself in the gloom, the complete contrast to Norway.

Hotpants is one of Sheffield's more colourful nightclubs. To the sound of seventies' music played at overpowering volume we discussed the results of our trip to Norway. The trip had been a success, as it was clear our plan was feasible. With hard work and a lot of luck we would be going again to the land of ice and snow the following year. Within a week the slides arrived. Everyone connected with the expedition turned up to see what they were getting themselves into.

With more confidence than I felt, I outlined the plan, answered questions and 'sold' Norway. As I looked at the slides, once more my mind travelled across the North Sea, up the fjords and on to the ice. There it stayed. Every day I dreamed of walking across the ice, of being able to see into the distance, up to the horizon and beyond.

After postponing the trip for a year I got in touch immediately with our sponsors. With extreme faith they all agreed to carry forth their support to the following year. Some even believed the decision showed sound leadership qualities as we were prepared to say that at the moment things weren't ready. Far too many expeditions push on regardless, resulting in a failed trip at best.

I had just under ten months to finalize the team, procure the majority of our equipment and consolidate the overall plan. At the time it seemed long enough. Yet problems take no heed of time, and we were to have plenty of problems in the following months.

4

BRICK WALLS AND BANGING HEADS

If the fool would persist in his folly he would become wise.
Blake

The smell didn't bother me too much. What got to me the most was the face being peeled down and the head being sawn in two, the top lifted off and the brain being extracted.

For some strange reason I was watching a post-mortem at the hospital where I was working as an auxiliary nurse. At the time it seemed a better way to make ends meet than teaching. By the skin of my teeth I had passed the teacher training course in Bedford. Norway had taken over my life. Although only a small expedition, everything was geared towards it. Due to the shift work involved in nursing I usually had either the morning or afternoon to work on the expedition. Yet on the afternoon after the post-mortem I did very little; come to think of it I did very little all that week.

After our return from Norway most of the sponsorship was procured. All our money came from corporate sponsorship, either locally or in some cases nationally. Once I'd begun writing letters which people could read, I normally received one letter in ten back with a positive reply. After speaking to Mick Coyne, all letters were one A4 side long, they asked for a specific amount of cash and stated for what it was to be used. Every letter was accompanied by a brochure. Once written to, each company was phoned up and pestered. Rather than writing to anyone, I only wrote to personal contacts or someone connected with the disabled. In the current economic climate you have to target suitable companies if you want them to pay for your obsession. For that's what expeditions are, an obsession.

Equipment was easier to secure. The only hard items to find were two long-wheelbase Land Rovers, sledges and radios. We hadn't decided on skis as no one could ski. Clothing and all the essential items, such as cooking kit, we gained from schools and youth groups all over the local area. Unless you are a big name in the expedition world or are planning a massively stunning expedition, it is of little use writing to the big and well-known outdoor firms. As a result the less well-known, would-be explorer has often to rely on sub-standard equipment.

However, equipment and money aside, the most important aspect to any expedition is the people who go on it. It was this side of the venture which was to generate all the problems in the forthcoming months.

In order to be within safe limits we would need at least six people to make the crossing. Two people needed to be with our wheelchair-bound person at all times. One person was to be with the visually-impaired person all the time, which left one person free to float between the two groups. Each group would be roped up independently and have one experienced person assigned to it. Supporting the ice-cap team would be two Land Rovers, each one with two drivers.

When we came back from Norway, I had eight people all interested in coming and happy with their assigned roles on the expedition, however, experience had taught me that these might well slip away like sand through the proverbial hourglass.

Dave Quarry had been confined to a chair for about two years. No one knew why he was paralysed from the waist down. All the tests had failed to reveal a cause. In response to my adverts in the various disabled publications, Dave came forward to join the expedition. Right from the start it was clear he was determined, fit and an extremely gutsy young man. He relished the idea of going to cross some distant ice-cap, although a little puzzled as to how he was going to achieve it. Like all people I have met who are confined to a chair as a result of an accident, Dave did not see himself as disabled.

Unlike Dave, John Sanders had been on similar ventures to the Norway expedition before. He had crossed Canada, been on an Outward Bound course and taken part in the Duke of Edinburgh's Award Scheme. Registered fully blind, he also seemed an ideal candidate for the trip.

My only criteria for selection was that people should first be able to pay £300, secondly that they were keen and thirdly that they were committed to the trip. As time wore on, the third point rapidly became the most important quality and the Achilles' heel of the expedition.

Like ice in the midday sun, a dream can melt away. So it was with Norway. Although the majority of the expedition was in place, I was to spend the remaining months trying to keep the team together.

In my mind there are two types of leader on an expedition. On one side there is the leader who is ideally suited to making decisions in the field. In contrast to the field leader is someone who is better suited to leading prior to departure. Unfortunately, I was better suited to leading the expedition in the field. My Cranwell training lent itself better to such a task. I am terrible at organizing. Things had been fine whilst the expedition had been a one-man band, yet as soon as other people became involved I became caught up in a never-ending cycle of crisis management and expedition politics.

Sue Dawson came to my rescue. In much the same way that Robert Swan got his expedition to Antarctica, leaving Roger Mear to get them to the South Pole, Sue got us to Norway. Hopefully, I was to get us back safely from the ice-cap.

Things began to go wrong at the first meeting after our reconnaissance trip. Mark and his girlfriend couldn't make it as they were in the process of moving house. Unfortunately, they couldn't get in touch and right from the start Sue didn't trust them. This began to lead to two camps in the expedition, those who came to the first meeting and those who did not. From my point of view I knew that Mark was completely committed to the expedition. Things came to a head when Sue refused to go if Mark went. It seemed irrelevant in her mind that she had never even met Mark. I couldn't tell Mark that he was dropped from the team as I had given my word. Unfortunately the other team members realized that something was afoot. People were confiding in Sue rather than me. It was a classic leadership failure.

Finally, Mark backed out along with his girlfriend, Rochelle. From my point of view this was a let off. I'd kept my word and had been saved from making a very awkward decision.

At the time Sue was undergoing her final year reading geography at York. She lived in a tiny caravan ten miles from the town. The stress of her degree, living conditions and picking up the pieces after me grew too much. With three months to go she backed out of the expedition. Events were happening at a frightening pace. I knew that other people on the expedition would see Sue's dropping out as a sign of lack of faith in my leadership. I was right.

Early one evening I drove up to York in a vain attempt to change her mind. All I achieved was coming close to getting thumped and losing her friendship for good. Tact has never been my strong point.

Within twenty-four hours of Sue dropping out Dave Harrison, one of the Land Rover drivers, had also backed out. This was doubly unfortunate as Dave was also providing one of the vehicles. Our sponsor had just agreed to pay the hire costs on the second Land Rover, knowing we had one already. The fact that we had just lost one made them also lose confidence. I felt like a man trying to take an ice-cube into the jungle. When I started it had been a large block of ice. If I wasn't careful all I'd have to show for a year and a half would be a damp cloth.

In order to achieve our aim I needed at least ten people. I was down to five. Five worried people with little or no experience in ice travel.

It was a worried young man who went round to Ted Grey's house one Saturday morning during the Easter break. At the end of the week we were due to have our first training trip. It was vital I went to the Lakes confident that the expedition was going to happen. At the moment I wasn't sure.

Ted Grey is the secretary of the Young Explorers' Trust. He was to provide crucial advice to the expedition over the coming months. That dull morning at Easter we formed a contingency plan which would enable us to go to Norway with only six people. 'Think sideways,' I had recently read. Think upside down, left and right, standing on one foot, I thought.

The training weekend was meant to be testing time geared towards selecting the most suitable members. However, following recent events I figured it would be wiser to put on a more relaxed affair. By trial, error and blind stubbornness I was getting the hang of pre-expedition organization.

Buttermere in the English Lake District provides a remote enough situation yet at the same time is close enough to civilization if something should go wrong. It soon became apparent that everyone going to Norway would have to be prepared to look after the disabled contingent before themselves. Over two days we learned what it was like to cope with disabilities in a mountain environment. All camp chores took at least twice as long, travel averaged at least three times the normal rate, and that was in a relatively safe situation.

Apart from forgetting the tent pegs and losing the minibus keys things went well. Over the weekend I put forward the revised plan. Bearing in mind the experience of our team, the size of group and having only one vehicle I explained, the plan was now to cross the ice-cap along its width. We would still be crossing the ice-cap yet, I believed, in a manner much better suited to the team. And with our aims still intact.

Everything considered, I was pleased with this adapted plan. No one else would drop out, would they?

I couldn't believe it. Claire, one of the team members, decided that if we weren't going to attempt the whole crossing then she didn't really want to go. She spoke to her brother who holds numerous qualifications in outdoor pursuits. 'Look, Claire, this Bull fellow has no qualifications, things aren't going well, and to top it all he's a bit of a cowboy.' This wasn't exactly the type of reputation I needed.

In order to halt the slide towards failure a big local recruitment campaign was put into action, during which Dave Quarry decided that he couldn't really trust anyone else to take him up to the ice-cap. He explained that he trusted the team so far because we had proved competent in the Lakes. In a way this was a blessing in disguise. It was also extremely sad as Dave would have got a lot more out of the trip than the person we actually took across the ice-cap.

Events were happening at an alarming rate. To console myself I read books by our patron. Even Ran Fiennes had problems. Nothing is impossible, I thought.

With one month to departure six people met in my local pub to discuss the final push.

At the eleventh hour Mick Barnes, an engineer, arrived to complete the team. Of similar age to my father he was an experienced skier and had sailed around Greenland. His maturity and experience in all areas of life were to be a bonus. At first I had doubts about his ability to mix in with a much younger team, yet the fact that he knew the infamous Bill Tillman convinced me to take him.

Zelda Garner is a music student and climber. During a particularly legendary night at the Plough in Hathersage, Zelda found herself the victim of two drunken young men expounding the virtues of Norway. Displaying either great courage or extreme stupidity she agreed to come on the expedition.

Helping with the backup team was John Brimble, registered fully disabled due to severe asthma. John managed to procure most of our camera film. For him the expedition was a first, having never been out of the country before. Norway was an age away.

Paul Jessop, retail manager for Iceland PLC, heard about the trip through Sue. A good friend of John Brimble, he seemed an ideal choice to partner J.B. on the backup team.

John Sanders I have mentioned earlier, and, as we sat in the pub seemed happy with the expedition and what we aimed to do.

At this stage in the final run to the trip I envisaged no real problems within the team. My only concern was that although everyone had been given specific areas of responsibility, no one had really done anything apart from John Brimble and Sue. However, once on the expedition this was to change.

Everyone had paid up, everyone had signed the insurance disclaimer which removed most of the responsibility from me if things went wrong, all were happy with their roles and everyone knew the aims and objectives. We all knew the plan to attain the objective. Before I knew it, there was only one week to go and all the kit began arriving at Fountaindale School where I was now working.

For one week life was chaos. My mind swam with doubt. Had everything been done? Had I forgot anything? One aspect of the expedition began to worry me; actually crossing the ice-cap. This may seem surprising or even foolhardy yet, to me it was very real. For a long time all I was concerned with was putting us into a position to actually go to Norway. True, I had a basic plan, yet it was now time to think seriously about the route across Jostedalsbreen.

With two days to go I taught my last lesson at school. Fountaindale is a special school catering for children with severe disabilities. It is a fantastic place to work and be involved with. All the children knew what I was aiming to do; indeed, they had all had turns at towing the pulks up and down the corridors. As I sat sorting the skis out one of the children came up to me. The child in question is confined to an electric chair, she can barely move her hands and can only just speak. With difficulty she handed me a card. 'Best of luck in Norway, love Kirsty.' In an instant I knew all would be well, I would carry the card across the ice.

5

OVER THE GREAT BLUE SEA AND BEYOND

If a man will begin with certainties, he shall end in doubts;
but if he will be content to begin with doubts,
he shall end in certainties.
Francis Bacon

Finally, everything came together early on the morning of Saturday, 2 July 1994. All the pressure and hassles of the previous months were blown away in the cold air of early morning. Underneath the school canopy stood a gleaming white Land Rover; strapped on top there lay four pulks. What with the stickers on the side proclaiming who we were, it cut quite a dash.

The dream which had begun out of desperation many moons ago actually seemed to be happening. I pinched myself and remembered we had to be in Newcastle by twelve to catch the ferry. Knowing my luck, something would go wrong on the way. Right up until everyone was on the vehicle I wouldn't be happy; the expedition had been dogged by people dropping out. It wouldn't surprise me if someone didn't turn up.

My pessimism was unfounded as all team members turned up on time and raring to go. Yukon Ho! We were off. Goodbye, dear old England, see you soon.

This is what life is about, driving off to take part in some adventure in some far-flung foreign country. Well, not quite far-flung but so it seemed to me as we speeded up the A1. The journey to Newcastle was uneventful, however, for the life of us we couldn't find a petrol station in North Shields. We asked several local people where we might find one; we had more success with Norwegian locals.

I was dreading the ferry journey. Not being the best of sea travellers I always indulge in too much beer, at least then I can put my illness down to something other than motion sickness.

So far, both Johns had been no problem. An onlooker would not have realized we had two disabled people with us. Our aim was integration; at an early stage in the expedition the team was fully integrated and getting on well with one another. The nature of the disability of the person you are taking on a trip decides whether or not you allocate a full time carer to that person. In our case we organized a rota so that at any one time there was always someone to look after John Sanders.

Within two hours of boarding the good ship *Venus*, three of our number were confided to bed due to the inevitable sea-sickness. In most cases there would be nothing unusual in this fact, however, when the sea is akin to the proverbial millpond I had doubts concerning the toughness of our team. The remaining three of us sat on deck staring back to a fast disappearing England. Unlike flying there is still something romantic about sea travel. In an age where you can jump on a plane and arrive on the other side of the world in twelve hours, travelling by sea is a throw-back to the days of Scott and Shackleton. Spending time on a ship, steaming along, increases the adventure and anticipation of the task ahead. As the ship rolled and rocked in the North Atlantic swell my mind skipped ahead to the mountains of central Norway.

How would John, registered fully blind, cope with the rock and ice of Jostedalsbreen? And John Brimble, would his lungs stand up to the exertion of the climb? At the time there was no answer to these questions. They remained a mystery just like the depths of the sea we were travelling across.

It seems strange now looking back on the expedition. My thoughts on the ferry to such problems were new. Most of the time prior to the expedition had been concerned with just getting us to Norway. True, the basic plan to get us across the ice had been worked out, but not in detail. As the time of reckoning approached my mind lay feast to a thousand worries and potential disasters.

Without great mishap we arrived in Bergen as sea mist rolled up the fjords, showing fleeting glimpses of distant ice. We were now in the land of polar heroes, Amundsen and Nansen. We were but little boys off to play in the giant's garden, yet what a garden!

Paul drove us off the boat, despite all good intentions and a terrible map we went completely the wrong way. Inbound for Bergen at thirty kilometres was not the start I had planned. After much profanity we found the right route and headed north.

An open road, the sun beating down, Bruce Springsteen drowning out the engine, distant memories of a beautiful girl and the prospect of adventure ahead — was there more to life? At that precise moment there wasn't.

Everything was going to plan. Originally we had planned to camp just outside Bergen, however, flexibility is the key to every successful expedition. Being flexible we headed towards Voss, aiming to put in as much mileage as possible.

The roads towards Voss are quiet and empty. After driving through tunnel after tunnel occasionally getting a glimpse of stunning mountains one finally reaches the Skegness of Norway. Voss is something of a shock really. One would expect a quaint little village, which it is in a way, apart from the tourists.

Being the premier ski resort in Norway, Voss attracts people. It didn't need more people, least of all us. We posted our postcards and headed further north aiming to reach Vangsnes by nightfall.

It is at about this stage in a travel book that the author either writes about the splendid country they are travelling through or relates other similar ventures.

The only reference to other expeditions I have so far made is to those of Wright, Croft and Fiennes. Yet, none of these eminent explorers have involved disabled people. In fact there are very few references to integrated expeditions. Jack Vander Molen led the Iceland Break Through expedition in 1986 in which a team of able-bodied and disabled explorers travelled through Iceland. Unfortunately Jack passed away recently, yet the Paul Vander Molen Foundation continues to carry out excellent work for the budding disabled explorer. John Hawkridge walked to Everest base camp suffering from cerebral palsy, showing the world that having a disability is not a problem. However, little has been written down as to what problems we might encounter. It was to be uncharted country for most of our team. Most expeditions experience enough problems in an extreme situation, so how would our group manage with both the environment and the added responsibility of coping with disabled people?

In terms of the country, the words I can put down on paper would not do justice to what we saw. I cannot comment on the people or the culture to any great extent as I paid most of my attention to worry and anticipation. I suppose in this way I am a failed travel writer as I have no record of the culture we experienced. There were more pressing things to mind.

At the last minute Ted Grey suggested we try to get hold of one of the new Global Positioning Systems (GPS). We arrived at Vangsnes to find ourselves the proud owners of a Norwegian chalet hut. Once unpacked and settled in I sat down and tried to remember how to use the GPS.

Most people believe PE teachers have more brawn than brains. I can tell you for a fact that this rumour is true. Ted and I had tried out the GPS in the Peak District. Utilizing several defence satellites spinning around the globe, it obtains a fix to within twenty-five metres, or should do. With little success at first, we had finally mastered it. Now as the time of reckoning approached I couldn't remember how to programme it. In England one enters in the OS system, however, in Norway one has to use either UTM or lat./long. With little luck I tried to use UTM, the Norwegian grid system; finally I tried lat./long. I had marginal success, yet it gave our position as being somewhere in the middle of the fjord near by. (At least I was getting the right planet which is more than Ted and I had got on Bleaklow.) This was quite perturbing as I was hoping to use the GPS as an accurate back-up to my navigation. The fault lay with the operator and not the equipment. I was confident that in time I could figure it out.

In Norway it is actually as cheap to stay in huts as it is to camp. We therefore spent an excellent night overlooking the Sognefjorden. Snowcapped mountains glinted in the distance and all was well.

The expedition was a full day ahead of schedule. We had experienced no major problems and everyone was looking forward to the challenge ahead.

Approaching Jostedalsbreen from the south, one catches the ferry from Vangsnes and heads up the Fjaerland fjord. Slowly as the ferry chugs up the fjord the ice-cap comes into view. Rising out of the water itself there stands a bastion of ice, larger than any in mainland Europe. All eyes on board the tiny ship are strained in an attempt to see more. Our eyes were straining more than most as we sought to identify our route up into the heavens.

At first the area looked completely different from the previous year; it looked alien and forbidding. Glancing around our team, it appeared they were thinking the same. After closer inspection through my pre-First World War binoculars the difference was obvious. Snow. Lots of snow covered the whole area where the hut was. The previous year the snowline had been much higher, now it extended half-way down the mountain.

Such a volume of snow could be either good or very bad. On one hand what crevasses there were may be completely covered in, therefore making the crossing a lot safer. However, if the weather had been warm then there would be a thin snow covering over the crevasses. This would make our journey a little more hazardous.

There was no time to ponder such possible problems as our ferry began docking and our presence was required to drive our rather overloaded vehicle off and on to the road, to strike yet more fear in the locals' hearts.

Boyabreen tumbles down from the Jostedal in a chaotic jumble of ice and snow. The year before we had stood on a nearby peak and listened with fascination as great blocks of ice broke away and blasted down the glacier. This time we stood below it on our way round the ice-cap to view the descent we would take on our completion of the trek.

There was an uncanny silence in the Land Rover as for the first time the scale of our undertaking sunk in. If our team was that of experienced and competent able-bodied mountaineers then it would have been different. A good analogy to our task in terms of mountaineering, was that we were taking into the mountains a team which most people would call out the rescue services for if they found themselves in our situation. In simple terms we were putting ourselves up the creek without a paddle. I didn't know whether everyone else felt this by then but as leader it was as apparent to me as the ice tumbling down into the valley.

6

THE UNDISCOVERED COUNTRY

An expedition's aim is best achieved by individuals who can look after themselves, need little or no directing or nursing.
Ranulph Fiennes

With more luck than we could have hoped for, we found a dirt track leading half-way up the mountain. The lesser distance we would have to travel on foot over rough terrain was a bonus. Our training trip had revealed that it would take at least twice as long to move over ground with a visually-impaired person. Thanks were offered all round to the Norwegian road builders, therefore, as we drove up the Befrings Valley to take a peek at our descent route.

Due to only receiving our Land Rover a day before departure none of us had any experience at all of off-road driving. Not that we were off road, yet the small, steep dirt track felt very 'off-roadish' to us.

Putting our hearts back where they belonged instead of in our mouths, we climbed out to be greeted by a cauldron of scenery. All around us steep granite walls rose up only to be capped by snow. In the distance lay the great white expanse of the ice.

Six small flies moved very slowly across a carpet of rocks and vegetation. The sun beat down and, in contrast the snow and ice reached down in an attempt to entice the flies into its grasp. In time two of the flies moved away from the others and moved up into the haunting vista. There they stayed for some time.

If someone had been looking down on us they would surely have seen what looked like flies. Leaving the Land Rover behind we pushed on up to get a better view of our likely descent. Alpine in

Mark Shearer in the early morning light above Fjaerland. *S. Bull*

The Flatbrehytta glacier, clearly presenting a problem for wheelchair users. *S. Bull*

Higher up the Flatbrehytta glacier. *S. Bull*

Union Jacks, ice-caps and a lone figure. *Boys' Own* here we come. ***S. Bull***

Clair Lancaster and Zelda sort out kit on the training trip. Note stretcher for access.
S. Bull

Anything is possible! Dave Quarry and John Sanders exploring the Lake District.
S. Bull

The original team that soon diminished. Paul Jessop centre with John Brimble far right.
S. Dawson

John Sanders and Steve Bull at the start of the crossing. *M. Barnes*

Jostedalsbreen ice-cap at last. *S. Bull*

Steve checks the team's position on the GPS. Deep wet snow hampered walking somewhat. *M. Barnes*

A timeless place of snow and ice. *S. Bull*

Finally the upper reaches of Flatbrehytta! *S. Bull*

After many hours on the move the team needed the odd rest. *S. Bull*

For Queen and Country and old fashioned adventure. *M. Barnes*

Striding into the sunset. *S. Bull*

A successful, yet tired team relax at the Flatbrehytta hut. *S. Bull*

Steve sorting out equipment before the Folgefonn ascent. *M. Barnes*

John Brimble on the bleak expanse of Folgefonn. *S. Bull*

Looking north across the ice to mountain upon mountain. *S. Bull*

Steve Bull.

M. Barnes

character the Befrings Valley provides somewhat easy access on to the ice-cap. Although Alpine in aspect the peaks are smaller in scale, the highest being only 1,544 metres.

There was a discussion in progress between Mick and Zelda, considering the weather forecast which was only good for the following week. Instead of driving back round to the Flatbrehytta hut and glacier and, effectively spending the next week training and moving gear on to the ice-cap as planned, the war council thought it was best to attempt the crossing from this side of the ice.

Jostedalsbreen is renowned for its bad weather. If the mist descended whilst we were half-way across then our work might be cut out. We needed to minimize every conceivable risk due to the limitations and nature of the team. One bonus in a crossing from the Befrings side was the fact that we would be descending into a known area which I would recognize. This might be a critical point in our favour if things went wrong. On the minus side of the revised plan was that we would be ascending a route unseen. To the able-bodied expedition this presents no great problem, yet for us it would be 'undiscovered country'. Secondly, and more worrying on a leadership point, was the reduced training time available to us. In order to dash through the window of good weather we needed to be on the ice in the next two days. This left the alarming prospect of only one day's training as opposed to the week originally planned.

After much consideration and consultation the decision was made to go from our current position. The weather swayed us. An expedition can plan every aspect, work out every detail, yet it can't control the weather. And, more often than not it is the weather that determines the overall outcome of the expedition.

Driving down the mountain was even worse than going up. Down in the valley nestling in the shadow of the gods we found the perfect chalet. Sitting on the wooden veranda all one could see was the sweeping vista of the mighty ice-cap.

The world was at peace and everything was still in the cool evening air. Unfortunately such tranquillity did not mirror itself in my mind. As the curtain-call approached John Sanders also seemed to become more aware of the challenge ahead. In being flexible we had changed the rules slightly. In the morning a suitable piece of snow needed to be found on which to practise the rudiments of glacier travel. Our equipment needed to be sorted out and the route planned.

Mick walked in from the shower having frozen himself under the 'fresh' jet of water. Whilst attempting to defrost he'd met another Briton. This being the first, it was cause for conversation. It transpired that Mike Gibbons had crossed the ice-cap way back in 1969 and had climbed the route we intended to use. Mike was amused to hear Ran Fiennes was our patron, relating somewhat humorous tales of a lecture Ran had given. Lady Luck had smiled on us again. By providing us with first-hand knowledge of the route on to the ice our worries eased.

Whilst down in the valleys John Sanders was at ease. We had experienced no real problems. John could shower, dress and toilet himself completely independently. However, there were perturbing signs, footnotes in a plot that was to unwind to near disaster over the following few days.

Mick was busy sorting out the general equipment, John Brimble and Paul were engaged with our food and fuel and the logistics of the backup team, Zelda busied herself with the clothing and I was in deep concentration planning the route. Unnoticed went the inability of John to pack his rucksack and sort out his own equipment. Unnoticed went the growing lines of doubt on John's brow. Like paint under a flame little cracks appeared. Yet the canvas was large enough for them to go unnoticed.

Using the GPS as backup I planned to navigate mainly by map and compass. As I pored over the map it became all too apparent how hazardous our undertaking was. True, if we were a group of friends heading up into the hills then the responsibility would be shared and accepted. Yet, the scenario was different.

As darkness crept slowly up the valley our preparations drew to a close. In the morning we would climb into the sun, snow and adventure.

7

THE WING OF A PRAYER

Now change the scene and let the trumpets sound,
for we must rouse the lion from his lair.
Old Play

Last minute additions to the kit were made. Gear was shared out amongst Zelda, Mick and myself. John Brimble and Paul, the backup team, were to accompany us to the hut, escorting John up. They would then descend leaving the four of us ready for our crossing. It was the Wednesday. If we hadn't arrived at the Flatbrehytta hut by first thing Monday morning then Paul was to alert the rescue services. Allowing a day to climb up to the ice-cap we planned to take two to three days to cross, leaving a day for bad weather. Taking five days' food, this allowed for a realistic schedule.

As the twentieth century draws to a close man has explored the vast majority of planet Earth. An expedition may set out arguing they are completing the last great challenge. Yet, these days many 'last great challenges' are a variation on a theme. No one will ever be the first to cross Antarctica again, or scale Everest. The North Pole has been reached and the South by motor bike, the Sahara crossed by wheelbarrow and the seas by windsurfer.

Parallel to this there is a great dam about to burst. A flood has built up which is about to open up and refresh the expedition field. People with disabilities are fresh to the exploring community. True, there have been a few people over the years who have been the exception to the rule, but by and large 'disabled' people have not been a part of exploration. The realities of this are staggering. Every expedition which integrates disabled people into the team will be achieving an expedition first. Every expedition. Disabled people are no different from the rest of us. We all have disabilities to some degree.

In 1900 the exploration of Antarctica lay ahead, untouched and virgin, anything was possible and all of it new. In the mid 1990s the integration of disabled people into private adventurous and scientific expeditions is just the same.

So it was on a bright sunny morning in central Norway — fresh, new and very exciting. The wild open spaces beckoned to feet that were shy and hampered by society. It was truly undiscovered country.

Again we had driven up the valley to a height of 700 metres in our Land Rover. The ice-cap began at a height of 1,500 metres, give or take a few metres. We should have arrived at a small hut on the edge of the ice-sheet in the early evening, in theory.

With a grunt and a groan I shouldered my rucksack. In Iceland I had carried ninety pounds. My present sack seemed somewhat heavier. It was certainly bulkier with a sledge strapped to the back. Using two ski poles for balance I set off. Zelda and Mick were coping well and likewise both Johns and Paul. Making steady progress we moved through the lower pastures. Even with loads on our backs the three of us moved markedly faster than the support team and John Sanders. This was nothing new as our training trip had revealed the extra time needed in travelling over rough ground. Despite this, all was going as planned.

I have yet to come across someone who enjoys walking uphill with heavy weights on his back. I certainly do not. At least my personal training programme had paid off. Prior to a trip I avoid carrying any rucksack of reasonable size, for this only serves to remind me of how hard it is to carry such sacks. Once on the trip one has no choice but to get on with the job in hand. Mike Stroud once remarked that the only reason he kept going back to the Arctic was due to the fact he couldn't remember how bad it all was. The key to being a well-known explorer is having a bad long-term memory.

Gradually, like ants moving across the garden lawn, we made our way up into the sun. It was taking longer than anticipated. It was one thing for John to walk confidently around Buttermere and through the Peak District, it was quite another prospect for him to move over ground similar to that of an untidy giant's bedroom floor. John Brimble was also moving slowly, yet this was understandable considering the state of his lungs.

We had frequent 'scenery' breaks. Well, to be honest, rest stops. Whilst indulging in numerous pit stops it gave us the chance to savour our surroundings. In every direction as far as the eye could see there lay mountains. Above us circled a bird, a golden eagle, watching our progress with amusement. It probably mistook us for insects, such was our painful progress. Bored with us it glided away into the distance and over the ice.

Time ticked away slowly but surely. The vista of stunning scenery which surrounded us blurred into insignificance as the desire to get to the top overcame everything else. In the early evening light we topped out on a col which led up to the summit. The alleged hut was only 300 metres above us. According to the map that is.

Our eagle had gone and along with it our energy and fresh legs. With great enthusiasm I deposited my rucksack on the snow and put it on to the sledge. We had been on the go for over ten hours.

A snow slope now lay between us and the prospect of a glorious night's rest. To both sides of the ridge we were on stretched fantastic open spaces, down in the valley nestled tiny Lego houses and the evening sun danced and sparkled on the forbidding crevasses beneath us. Adopting by now our customary slow pace, we inched up the slope. It soon became apparent that the slope was going to present something of a problem. Almost immediately we had to dump our loads and haul them up by rope. At fifty metres a go this became time-consuming and exhausting. To compound this, both Johns were moving very slowly. In John Brimble's case the effects of the climb up were now taking their toll. Although our altitude was not great his lungs were gradually failing him. John Sanders also found himself in a situation that was both new and dangerous. Having the most obvious drawback of no sight, every single step was now an adventure.

Bearing in mind the relative experience of the team and the nature of the disabilities, we were walking a thin tightrope between disaster and success.

A sense of urgency infected us all. Night was closing in around us, quickly and unwelcome. It speeded our thoughts and galvanized our tired limbs into action.

Mick and Paul began moving gear on up to the illusive hut, Zelda set about making a depot of the sledges and all unwanted gear for the night and I roped up our two Johns. The spectre of accident and the following failure of the expedition proved to be the catalyst which got us all safely into the hut, perched fantastically overlooking scenery one dreams about.

As everyone moved over the final boulder field to our sanctuary I checked the sledges a final time. It wouldn't do to wake up the next morning only to find them somewhere down in the valley. All things considered, the team had done extremely well. True, we hadn't broken any speed records, yet all were safe and well and the goal achieved. Staring out into the setting sun my mind wandered and followed my glare. 'A cry of lamentation for days which have had their trial and failure, and have left deep traces of it which the blind may see.' Charles Dickens seemed to capture the efforts of six mortals climbing out of a valley on to high snowy ground. The eagle looking down on us would not have seen four able-bodied 'normal' people, one blind man and one disabled man. It would simply have seen six figures, six insignificant small dots moving slowly, in a land that would regard their presence as would a giant regard a fly crawling across his face. But most of all it would have seen the six figures as equal. For on the climb we had all been equal: integrated and equal. If the expedition achieved no more it would still be a success.

Cold crisp wind woke me from my daydreams; like the sinking sun my cigar too faded away. Turning my back on the approaching darkness I moved quietly up the snow to join the others.

In stark contrast to the pure air we had been breathing all day the hut was stuffy and humid. Due to the lateness of our arrival, Paul and John spent the night in the hut with the rest of us. John Brimble was now paying in full for his efforts during the day. In fact, all of us were thoroughly exhausted. It wasn't long before the wooden walls echoed to the sound of deep sleep and snoring.

8

THE CROSSING

I did not know what I was capable of but I knew that I was no loser. Maybe I was born to struggle, but not to accept defeat. I am British; English and furthermore a Yorkshireman.
John Hawkridge

Sunlight fell through the window bringing to life a myriad of tiny dust particles. They danced and sparkled alone for a while until the six inert bodies began to stir. Slowly all began to rouse themselves to face the prospect of another glorious day. After the previous day it seemed sensible to rest and recuperate. After a breakfast of somewhat palatable freeze-dried food Paul and John Brimble set off down the hill. We waved them off as we retrieved the gear from the night before. Making a mockery of our exertions the previous day, they zoomed down the snow slope. It was as if the guardians of the ice were laughing at us. Paul and John faded into the morning sun as did the laughter. It was a glorious day. By lunch-time not only had we recovered our kit, we had also placed a depot on the very edge of the ice-cap. In order to gain access to the ice, one had to travel across another boulder field. We intended setting off the next day, and seeing that it would be hard enough with John, we carried all our gear the two kilometres across ground very similar to that of Scafell Pike. Snow had so far not presented a problem to John. Boulder fields, however, were a different ball game. I know from experience that it is quite possible to twist an ankle on such terrain. The dangers were somewhat increased if you couldn't see.

Having prepared all we could for our outing the next day

we now had a chance to savour our surroundings. Both Mick and Zelda were openly loving the situation. It was impossible to stare straight on to the ice-cap as the sun was so bright. What wasn't so bright at this stage was John's enthusiasm for the walk ahead. After the previous day, although tired, John was very quiet. As leader I should have noticed such signs, yet I was too excited by the adventure which faced us and wrongly assumed we all had the same desire to explore the great expanse of white ahead of us. Looking back now from my comfy chair in front of the word processor, I blame myself entirely for the problems which came within an ace of causing disaster. Like a schoolboy rushing home to begin his school holidays, I could think of nothing other than finally getting down to crossing the ice-cap.

For some reason we had been blessed with perfect weather. If anything it was a little too hot yet beggars can't be choosers. We spent the day checking our route and marking the compass bearings on the map. Unfortunately, I still couldn't figure out how to enter UTM into the GPS. Finally giving up I entered the lat./long. co-ordinates. The reading given wasn't the most accurate in the history of navigation. This was probably down to my shaky biro lines along the map rather than any fault with the GPS. After redrawing the lat./long. lines (this time in pencil) I got a better reading. With much relief I was confident the GPS could back up my own navigation.

Way back in 1898 Kristian Bing, the first person to cross the ice-cap had no such technology, yet I doubt he had tried to integrate a visually-impaired person into his team. The ice-cap has been crossed many times since those early days; even Ranulph Fiennes, our patron, had crossed it before he became a well-known name. However, as far as we know, it has never been crossed by an integrated team.

We basked in the sun like seals on a beach. The sun began to sink once again into the magical twilight that is common in summer. As it sank our excitement rose. In my dreams through the night the ice assailed me, endless hours of walking possessed me and the thought of taking three inexperienced people into the wilderness haunted me. Memories from the previous year came back; how would John cope with the crevasses and steep snow slopes? Sleep came and with it the point of no return.

Being where we were and about to do what we intended was a God-given privilege. Whilst writing this book I am teaching PE at Fountaindale School still. Earlier in the book I mentioned that Fountaindale caters for severely disabled children. I wish with all my heart that the children I teach could have experienced what we did in the high Norwegian sun. On one hand it is immensely rewarding teaching such children yet, on the other, it is very distressing. Kirsty will never be able to buy her own drink in a bar, never be able to walk through the woods we live in and never be able to feed herself. The mountains of Norway are as far away and as alien as the moon. Most of my friends fly fast jets, mine gold in Africa, patrol Bosnia or practise medicine. I would not trade places with any of them. To see our children smile is worth more than any gold or title. It was with these thoughts that I walked over the rough boulder field to the edge of the ice.

By dumping most of our gear the day before we had saved ourselves a great deal of time and effort. Mick and I went ahead to find the sledges and pack them whilst Zelda guided John over the rocks. Even at this point John had begun to retreat into himself. The problem was not a question of his disability yet simply one of personality. At that stage, where it was as easy to go on as go back, I believe he realized he had overextended himself. We had to make the most of the situation. I too was at fault. My single aim was now to cross the ice; if John didn't like it then so be it. He knew from the start what he was letting himself in for. This may all sound a bit harsh, I know, however, my aim is to document the expedition, warts and all.

There was no more planning to do, there was no more kit to pack, no more money to raise and no more problems to sort out. Life had become very simple. All we had to do was walk.

Picking a small bump on the horizon we strode off into the wide open expanse of Europe's highest ice-cap. I roped up John between Mick and Zelda. There was little danger of crevasses in the area, yet Sod's Law ruled that if we hadn't roped up someone would have fallen down one. At first I was amazed at how easy it was to pull a sledge along. We had put both John's and my kit in my sledge and Mick and Zelda pulled their own kit. We didn't use skis simply because only Mick could cross-country ski. Probably doing everything wrong in terms of manhauling, we tramped off into the morning sun.

Almost immediately I was forced into making a comparison between my sledge load and that of our patron as he walked across Antarctica. Mine probably only weighed about 150 pounds at most. It was hard to comprehend how Ran Fiennes could tow over 500 pounds for over ninety days.

We pulled up a snow slope for what seemed like for ever. In front of us lay the never-ending ice-cap. Well, from where I stood it looked never-ending. One look at the map confirmed it was only about eighty miles long. We must have been mad to contemplate taking someone in a chair across it. For a start there is no sledge system as yet designed to take a wheelchair-bound person across the polar wastes of the world. Behind us the mountains of central Norway slowly faded away. To our left and right yet more mountains slid past, a continuous screen of awesome scenery.

Only after a few hours of walking Mick came up to me to express some doubts that were building up. Storm clouds were massing behind us and John was also very quiet. These two concerns he voiced to me. Unfortunately I felt the same. Looking back now I believe John was scared; he had never been in such a situation before, and the reality of his situation had overwhelmed him. As a result he had withdrawn into himself. This was entirely my fault, of course. Due to not selecting people on how they could cope under stress I was now paying the penalty. There was also an added problem. Our tents were no better than Wendy houses. Again this was my fault. Not being able to secure tents through sponsors or companies specializing in outdoor pursuits I was forced to take what I could. As a result, the tents we had were ropy at best. They would stand up to bad weather down in the valley; up on the Jostedal things were somewhat different though.

A radical change of plan was therefore conceived on the high snow-covered plateau. Instead of spending several days crossing the ice we would attempt to do the trip in one big haul. To me this looked like another big epic in the offing. Yet, in reality we had little choice. Our tents would not stand up to what looked like an imminent storm and John was likely to crack just like our wooden tent poles. It was certainly feasible to get to the Flatbrehytta hut in one day.

All three seemed happy with the new plan. It wasn't ideal, however. Unlike a fully able-bodied expedition we could not afford to take any chances.

From looking at the map I figured that over the next rise we would see a long flat snowfield stretching out in the distance. As we walked over the rise my heart skipped a couple of beats. According to my eyes there was no such geographical feature in sight. What they did see was a mass of glaciers, mountains and very nasty looking crevasses. This was quite perturbing. As the others approached I got out my secret weapon. Positioning Resources to the rescue! However, due to my rather shoddy lat./long. lines the GPS gave our position as somewhat in the middle of one of the crevasse systems.

'Everything all right, Steve?' Mick enquired.

'Yep, no problem!'

With a certain amount of controlled haste I looked at the map again, with great relief I realized that I had been holding the map the wrong way up. The hairs which had risen on my spine slowly went down. Ahead of us lay a great expanse of white. Like a small ship on the distant horizon there lay a peak. It was this peak that we were aiming for. Hopefully, it marked the top of the Flatbrehytta glacier. And with it safety and security.

All this may sound extremely melodramatic and quite over the top, especially if you are anything like an experienced mountaineer. Yet, as leader of our small team I felt extremely vulnerable and exposed. I had confidently told John's mum that he would be in no real danger. This was somewhat of a white lie. Our distinct lack of training in the ice and snow department was causing me some concern, however, with thanks to my Cranwell training I was able to put on an outward show of confidence even though I didn't feel it.

Despite all these doubts it had to be said we were making good, steady progress. True, we weren't breaking any records, yet no one could deny the fact that we were out there doing the business. The expedition was real and happening. Life is for living, and at that precise moment, all four of us were involved in an adventure. For John it was probably the adventure of a lifetime.

9

DANCING IN THE DARK

We shall go always a little further: it may be beyond that last blue mountain barr'd with snow.
James Elroy Fletcher

Like invisible phantoms dancing in the dark on a black stormy night we moved unseen to the onlooking world. Slowly but surely we inched our way across the roof of the world. Time became as nothing, for all intents and purposes we could have been travelling through the very oceans of time. The ice we inched across had been there for an age; it would be there flong after our mortal frames had ceased to exist. As we walked along I thought of nothing. My automatic pilot steered me towards the white peak in the distance. My mind travelled out on to the ice and found a freedom in the lonely wasteland that surrounded me.

Far out over the horizon our eagle returned. It flew on a parallel course to our own, regarding us with strange curiosity.

As the eagle flew high up in its element it saw four black specks moving across a white blanket. If it had looked a little more closely it would have seen that they moved quite slowly. It would also have noticed that one figure travelled ahead of the other three and that the three were connected by what looked like a long worm. If at this stage it had examined the strange line a little more closely it would have noticed that one of the figures walked with head bowed, staring down at the whiteness they moved over. Every so often the group stopped when the three caught the one up. They normally stayed motionless for some time. Losing interest in this strange procession the eagle flew away; it had far better things to do with its time.

We were moving quite slowly as groups go. Although John wasn't towing any equipment his speed over ground was obviously slower than that of someone who could see. However, we took our time. Every so often we would stop and indulge in a hot drink and something to eat. Walking across such terrain is in reality very boring. I would often walk ahead of the main group preferring to travel at my own pace and then wait for the others to catch up. There was no danger in my doing this as the weather was still fine and the skies clear. As we walked along I worried constantly. I was concerned by the accuracy of our navigation, or to be more precise, my navigation. The GPS was giving readings that were probably half a kilometre out. This was assuming that my map reading was accurate. Although I had complete confidence in my map and compass work I wasn't sure whether the underlying rocks were affecting the compass or not. However, ignorance being bliss I chose to ignore this technical snag and plod on.

As the day progressed we gradually came to the end of the snow plateau we were travelling along. Directly in front of us lay a rather steep looking snow slope which in turn led up on to a col. Now, if my navigation was correct, beyond the col and down the other side lay the Flatbrehytta glacier.

Mick was concerned. He was concerned that the slope I intended moving up was too steep for us. True, from where we stood it did look a little on the steepish side. Yet, according to my now rather tatty map it was really only a gentle incline. Displaying more confidence than I felt, I announced that once on top of the col we would see the glacier we needed and from there the hut would be within our grasp.

The team were still working well together. Both Zelda and Mick were coping well with the pulling and seemed to be enjoying the experience. John on the other hand was extremely quiet. The reasons for this are hard to define. Since coming back from Norway I believe that he realized once on the ice-cap that he had overstretched himself. His reaction to this was simple, he withdrew from the situation in order to cope with it. This had little to do with his visual impairment but more his personality. However, the two are almost definitely linked.

As it turned out the snow slope was nothing more than a gentle incline. By this stage though our untrained limbs were steadily feeling the effects of many hours' walking over soft damp snow. Reaching the top of the col, I searched the horizon for the top of the glacier. Nothing. All I could see through the late afternoon glare was mountain upon mountain. Our eagle had gone long ago and at that moment the bleak expanse of Jostedalsbreen never seemed more lonely. Situations are never as bad as they first appear, and this situation was no exception. Only by walking a little way over the col was it apparent that I need never have worried about the navigation. Straight ahead and below us lay the great white river of Flatbrehytta. We had hit it spot on, all we had to do now was descend from the col we were on and from there it should be a walk in the park. Should be!

The previous year when Mark and I had carried out the reconnaissance trip we had found the descents from the peaks extremely suspect. It was with some trepidation then that I led our little band down the incline and towards the glacier. Yet again though, my worries were unfounded. Due to the large amount of winter snow, all the crevasses were covered in. In no time at all we were off the plateau and safely positioned on the upper reaches of the Flatbrehytta glacier.

At this stage all should have been well in my somewhat tiny mind, however, as I looked down the glacier it looked as alien as the moon. For the life of me I couldn't recognize one single feature from the previous year. This was a little worrying. The cause of this was twofold: in the first instance we hadn't come as far up the glacier the year before and, second, the large amounts of snow made everything look completely different. Once I realized these facts and had confirmed our position on the map I felt distinctly better.

Now for the first time in the trip I could afford a feeling of relaxation and satisfaction. True, the dangers weren't over but now I was on familiar ground. With this in mind we stopped on the upper reaches of the glacier to celebrate. By this stage both Zelda and John were becoming increasingly tired, and when tiredness sets in accidents can happen.

If our eagle had flown over us at that time he would have

experienced a strange and schoolboyish ritual.

The four figures had stopped altogether and formed a tight huddle on the vast expanse of the white river. On taking a closer look the eagle would have seen a multicoloured piece of cloth unfurl in the light evening breeze. The group moved around this cloth for some time. After a while they put the cloth away and moved off down the river that doesn't move.

We weren't really planting our flag for Queen and country, but in celebration of getting John across the ice-cap. Up till now we had done our best to integrate him fully into the team. Our Union Jack was flown in celebration of a new era in integrated expeditions.

The temperature was dropping just as surely as we were dropping in height. All day we had experienced warm sunny weather, yet as the sun sank below the mountain tops a cold wind blew up the glacier. Feeling the wind on my face and looking round at my team-mates I was completely content. The pulks glided over the snow and we saw no sign of any crevasses. In a couple of hours we should be in sight of the hut, safety and sleep. Although we felt we had done the worst of it the mountain was not yet ready to let us go. It had one last trial for us to undergo.

We discussed whether or not to spend the night on the ice, as by now both John and Zelda were suffering somewhat. Rightly or wrongly we opted to push on to the hut and with it a close brush with disaster and death.

10

STUMBLING TOWARDS THE CURTAIN OF NIGHT

You only live twice: Once when you are born
And once when you look death in the face.
Basho

I was hurtling down the slope rather too quickly for my liking. Zelda had gone first and then called me forward as she thought the slope looked a little too steep. Not bothering to unclip my pulk or put crampons on, I had confidently walked forward to assess the danger. Before I knew it the weight of my pulk pushed me over and down the slope. My ice-axe was safely packed in the pulk and not in my hand where it should have been. The only chance I had was to steer myself somehow towards some rocks to the side of me. With a crunch I hit the rock outcrop after some rather frantic steering with my feet. Rather shaken, I came to the conclusion that the slope was steeper than it looked and we would have to reconsider our final descent to the hut.

We were in imminent danger of experiencing another epic similar to that of our ascent. However, this time we were a lot more tired. As we sat at the top of the slope the wind whistled past us, an icy reminder that the day was drawing to a close. Confidently and quickly Zelda descended the slope. Not wanting to take any chances with John, I tied myself off to an ice-axe and roped him up for the descent. John chose this time of the day to switch off altogether. At the time I lost my patience with him as the temperature was dropping all the time. We could ill afford the delay. Looking back at the situation I now realize that John must have been very scared, to put it mildly. The situation was bad enough for us; John couldn't even see what he was letting himself into. Inch by inch John was lowered down to the safe patch of snow where Zelda was.

Now, on the way up the pulks had proved to be a bit of a snag. Not wanting to go through the same rigmarole, I came upon a faster way of getting them down. We retrieved the fifty metre rope from my sack, tied one end to the ice-axe and the other to all three pulks. With a swift kick the pulks were launched off down the hill. Immediately, it was apparent that it wasn't such a good idea. All three pulks tumbled over and over, narrowly missing Zelda and John. On they sped in their chaotic dance. With a snap the rope came taught and somehow held all our equipment. By repeating the process three more times we managed to get the pulks off the slope in record time, and then on to a ledge where they were safely depoted for the night.

Getting equipment down safely is one thing, for if needs be it can be left if things get too dire, yet getting a blind person down a steep snow slope after thirteen hours on the move is quite another prospect.

We now began to pay for our distinct lack of training in the ice and snow department. Zelda was fine as her rock-climbing experience paid off. John on the other hand was having extreme problems. After the initial slope I decided it was best to go unroped, mainly due to the speed factor and the lateness of the hour. Instead, Mick walked John down the final slopes to the hut. All the time coming down those final metres John would slip. His training hadn't been sufficient for him to remember the techniques when the pressure was on. By making the decision to go with the good weather we were now paying for it with interest. Mick lost count of the times he stopped John from taking the quick way down the hill and during the whole episode I think John hated us all, especially me for putting him there in the first place.

Finally though, the Flatbrehytta hut loomed out of the gloom. There was nothing either remotely dramatic or romantic in the completion of our crossing. John was hauled up to the hut literally by the scruff of his collar. Zelda was suffering from heat exhaustion, Mick was cursing John as if profanity was going out of fashion and

I was just thanking every single star above us for a safe if somewhat lucky deliverance.

Just like the year before, the hut was an absolute godsend. Hot drinks were served up all round before each one of us sulked away to our bags. Tired and exhausted, the tribulations of the day were left to take seed during a disturbed and troubled sleep.

Our eagle had long ago vanished into the silent wastes we had travelled over. Had he seen our final performance he would have laughed in quiet solitude at our efforts. They amounted to nothing more than schoolboy antics on the playing fields of life. Our eagle knew this, yet as we slept we were innocent to such truthful thoughts. It would only be later on that such musings would be raised, questioning the very philosophy of our expedition.

11

SOUR SUCCESS

We are not now that strength that in old days
Moved earth and heaven.
Tennyson

In the early morning light shadows of mountains danced off the Sognefjord some 4,000 feet below us. In the old and dark corners of the hut we slowly roused ourselves to face each other after the traumas of the previous evening. It was a glorious morning. Behind us the ice-cap lay silent and brooding, unmarked by our passage. Below us the fjord lay host to a thousand different dancing reflections, welcoming the dawn of another new day. The satisfaction of reaching the hut had faded away just as quickly as the early morning dew. In its place lay a growing feeling of anticlimax and the prospect of discontent within the ranks.

It was immediately clear that John was unhappy with the antics of the previous day. He wanted to go down, off the mountain and away from danger. The remainder of us wanted to spend the rest of our time in Norway exploring the ice-cap. This could create problems. Anyway, there was little we could do until the backup team arrived.

We sat above a great vista of stunning scenery waiting for John Brimble and Paul to ascend from the valley floor. There was still work to do as we had left the pulks on our descent the previous evening. Leaving John with strict instructions not to move from the hut, the rest of us climbed back up the ice slope to retrieve the equipment. Without incident we picked up the kit and returned to our base. As we did so the mist began to descend on the ice above us.

Like dragon's breath it floated silently down, cloaking everything in its mysterious clasp. With the great benefit of hindsight it seemed we had made the correct choice in crossing the ice-cap the way we had.

As we sat overlooking the fjord, the mist curled around us. Out of the dragon's breath there emerged a figure, a lone figure, hunched and struggling over each step. The figure grew larger, it slowly moved over patches of snow and disappeared between sporadic gusts of low cloud. Finally, without warning, John Brimble's face popped from around the corner of the hut. Happy, but pained. In a period of five hours he had climbed the mountain, closely followed by Paul. Without complaint they both sat down to a rather large mug of hot sweet tea.

If by chance our eagle had now flown over the hut he would have seen a larger group of small black dots, sitting huddled together, oblivious of all outside events. It would soon have become bored with the obvious sign of inactivity and flown off to find the dragon.

Our conversation was animated as we recalled our experiences of the last few days. In time the chat turned to what we were now going to do. There was still over a week and a half left of the expedition. Having completed our aim, there was a distinct danger that the following time would be wasted in a blaze of inactivity and anticlimax. Our current situation was ideal for Mick and Zelda who wanted to explore the world of ice further. However, for John Sanders it was not ideal. In his own mind he had done what he had come to do; he now wanted off the hill. Due to the nature of the expedition, we had only one course of action left to us, that of descending to the valley and finding some other activity which would involve all members of the expedition equally.

As leader, I began to turn my thoughts to an alternative plan. We packed our equipment and made preparations to leave the hill. As we cleared up Mick suggested we leave money in the hut to cover what I hadn't paid the previous year. I argued that we had little money as it was without paying for my errors of the year before. Ignoring me, Mick said he would leave some money of his own to keep the farmer happy. As we set off down the mountain I believed the debts incurred by Mark and myself were settled.

This was to be a potentially disastrous belief.

We awoke the next morning to a land shrouded in mist and rain. Our aim for the day was clear and simple, to get off the mountain. It had become clear the previous day that any further time spent upon the ice would not increase our integration philosophy. Preparations were therefore put in order to descend. All experienced mountaineers know that it is often the descent which is the most dangerous part in any climbing operation. Due to the now rather bad weather we needed to exercise speed in order to reach the valley safely. However, even this tactic was to put some of the members in jeopardy.

As on the climb up, Mick, Zelda and I concentrated on getting our pulks and gear down. Paul was left with John Brimble to escort John Sanders down, and in that order we struggled off into the gloom of a dull Norwegian day.

Over the initial steps I was transported back in time to the start, the start of my rather sporadic involvement in the outdoors. All I can remember is rain, lots of rain and plenty of mist on the dark and bleak expanse of Kinder Scout. My parents used to take me for long windy walks throughout the whole of Derbyshire. This led to the Lake District where upon I was dragged up most of Cumbria's mountains. Eventually though I rebelled as there was surely a more interesting way to spend one's Sundays and holidays than walking. However, in my late teens the call of the wild was distinct. A seven day journey along the Pennine Way reminded me that walking on its own was no fun. As a result, along with Dave Tait I embarked on the extremely stupid sport of rock climbing. I say stupid because when you're scared of heights as I am, climbing is stupid. After many an epic throughout England and Scotland it seemed that expeditions in a more general field seemed safer.

'Safe, this path is not safe!' I thought. And anyway, safe is a relative term, cave diving is relatively a lot safer than driving down the M1. In turn, driving down the motorway is safer than taking a blind person across an ice-cap.

All the pressure of what to do next in the expedition vanished almost immediately. Our path down the mountain was similar to the one that may be found on Great Gable descending to Windy Gap, steep and rocky, with plenty of places on it to fall a long way, unimpeded by earthly bounds. Right from the outset it seemed my pulk and rucksack preferred the faster option to the valley floor. This, however, was incompatible with my own personal feelings on the matter. Very soon all members of the expedition were left alone, to fend for themselves on the route down, come what may. Paul obviously stuck with both Johns, yet the rest of us became engaged in a battle of balance. Due to the nature of the path it was impossible to carry my load down on my back. Instead, rather like taking a dog for a walk, I tied my pulk and sack to a short climbing sling. With my load on a lead I proceeded to kick, pull and push the awkward weight down the hill.

My 'dog' unfortunately preferred steep snow to the rocky path it was supposed to stay on and, as a result, I suddenly found myself hurtling down the snow, heading for a rather steep cliff. Even before I had time to contemplate my fate I slammed into some wonderfully positioned rocks. I had words with my pulk and attempted to drag it back on to the path. All this time both Zelda and Mick looked on in amusement. They were not having the same problems as I was as their pulks were distinctly smaller.

Further down the mountain, similar antics were to be seen by any unsuspecting onlookers. Due to the rain the ground had now become very wet and slippery underfoot. As a result John Sanders was having a terrible time in trying to stay upright. Paul had his work cut out. Slipping and sliding down the hillside they managed by dint of good fortune to avoid any major accidents.

In terms of 'proper' leadership, my conduct down the hill was incorrect; it was quite simply every man for himself. With hindsight we should have relayed loads down the hill, making sure that everyone was safe first. Our luck was in with regard to walking down, yet it certainly was not in with regard to Norwegian farmers who owned mountain huts. As I staggered round a bend in the path there stood Eric Oygard!

My worst fears were confirmed almost straight away; not only did he recognize me, he also asked if I had the money from the previous year. I confidently told him that my friend had left some cash in the hut. He waved cheerio and bounded off up the mountain.

Praying that Mick had indeed left some money, I resumed my rather erratic walk downhill.

The last stage of the walk down to the valley follows a small track, laborious yet safe. My knees by this stage were beginning to complain. Every step sent shooting pains up my leg. Instead of walking, I broke into a small trot in order to end the pain sooner. What my friends further up the mountain were doing I had no idea for I had long ago left them. Somewhat akin to a wounded elephant crashing through the undergrowth, I pounded down on to the valley floor. There, standing like a vision of heaven was our Land Rover.

After calling Mick up on the radio, he confirmed that everyone was safely on the track and within half an hour of the finish. As soon as I knew that everyone was safe I relaxed, got a brew on and had a cigarette. Life is seldom any better.

My peace was suddenly shattered by a large four-wheel drive van pulling up. Out stepped a rather angry looking woman whom I recognized as the farmer's wife. Apparently Mick had not left any money in the hut which Eric the farmer soon discovered. Thinking he had been conned, he radioed his wife in order that she may intercept us. This she did. Eric's wife was in no mood to argue, if I did not pay her straight away she would call the police and have us arrested. I explained that my friend had all the money on him and that we would drive round and pay her as soon as he arrived. With luck, after offering her my Rolex watch as security, she trusted me. As she drove off I lit another cigarette and thanked our guardian angel.

Within the next few minutes a tired yet elated group of people wandered up to the vehicle. Wet, dirty and exhausted the Integrated Norway Expedition gathered around to drink hot sweet steaming tea. We had done it.

12

ODDS AND ENDS

A rusted nail, placed near the faithful compass,
Will sway it from the truth, and wreck the argosy.
Even this small cause of anger and disgust
Will break the bonds of amity 'mongst princes,
And wreck their noblest purposes.
The Crusade

A chill wind blew amongst us; the warm comforting breeze of success had blown away. Immediately after our descent from the ice-cap there had been a great feeling of satisfaction, not just because we had crossed the Jostedalsbreen, but also because we had managed to live up to our integration ideal. Yet once we had relaxed and sorted the gear out there was a general feeling of anticlimax. What would we now turn our sights on? Our aim and objective had been achieved in an almost clinical manner. In my plans I had not imagined having spare time as I had envisaged us taking the full three weeks to carry out the crossing.

As a reward for the hard work of the past few days we decided to spend a couple of days in the Land Rover driving around the Jotunheim National Park. In its own way this was both visually stunning and a welcome break from walking, however, it was hardly challenging.

Over yet another freeze-dried meal, a council of war was called. Mick and Zelda both wanted to have a bash at cross-country skiing. Everyone else was happy with whatever we did. Here though was an excellent chance for us to integrate our disabled team-mates even more. On the drive up from Bergen we had driven through a great plateau area just south of Voss. At the time this had been covered in snow and ice. Our plan was simple, to travel back to this area and conduct a programme of integrated skiing, camping and climbing. So we planned!

If nature is anything, it is unpredictable. Heavy rain lashed down from the heavens, effectively melting away all the snow from our proposed venue. The six of us sat, miserable and dejected, in a damp and cramped, sweaty Land Rover. What now? It was a time to be democratic. Did anyone have any ideas? No. What do you want to do now? Don't know. Mutterings about heading back to Bergen spread through the ranks. Mick wanted to take John Sanders back on the train and still the rain came down. The time for being democratic came and went.

'I've looked at the map and there appears to be a rather large lump of ice west of Bergen. We can be there by nightfall if we drive hard and fast. Once there we shall climb it, ski it and camp on it. Any objections? No? Good. Paul, pass me the Bruce Springsteen tape.'

With the winds at our backs and a purpose in our hearts we drove south. I'm sure the scenery was splendid and the weather fantastic yet I did not notice. We stopped once to eat and once to clean the Land Rover as John Sanders' dinner didn't agree with his stomach. By nightfall we sat camped by a deep blue lake under the shadow of ice and snow.

The Folgefonn ice-cap is the third largest in Norway and hence central Europe. It would provide the excellent opportunity for us to involve everyone on the mountain. We did not know it then but it would also be the setting for the virtual breakdown of our aim of integration.

In stark contrast to the bleak and wild expanse of Jostedalsbreen we were now camped amongst rolling green hills. A flat mirror of deep blue reflected all of nature's splendour in stunning clarity. At the top of the valley a great dragon lived, for all we could see was its steamy breath as it slept, unaware of our mortal presence. Every so often the dragon flew away, taking its misty breath with it. In its absence it left a gleaming white cap of pure and sparkling snow. Yet the dragon would return every morning from its nightly flights. It breathed down a constant stream of cloud and mist, preventing us from venturing into its lair. For two days we remained tentbound, enduring the only wasted days of the expedition due to bad weather so far. It was a testing time.

We passed the time playing endless games of cards and listening to the epic *Lord of the Rings* on the Land Rover's tape deck. After two days the weather cleared sufficiently for us to make an initial foray on to the lower ice slopes above us. As we drove up the steep and often scary minor road through the valley the Folgefonn ice-cap drifted out of the mist. Although a lot smaller than Jostedalsbreen, it is still large and forbidding. On the morning we approached it there was a soft covering of cloud swirling down from the summit. The dragon was close by.

Rather conveniently for us, the Norwegians had built a small ski slope at the bottom of one of the glaciers. Serving this little-known piste is a tiny wooden hut which provides skiers with any refreshment and advice that they may need. For us it was complete luxury.

At Christmas-time I had learnt to ski after a fashion at Zermatt. Using my own plastic climbing boots and a friend's mountaineering skis, I was introduced to the delights of downhill skiing. Displaying no style and an addiction to falling over I eventually got the hang of it. Now in Norway we donned our cross-country skis and set out to learn to ski the Norwegian way. Mick was the only one out of the group who could do this. The rest of us spent the time polishing our backsides on the smooth hard snow.

In theory, this should have been an ideal part of the expedition where we became fully integrated. Yet events were to prove us all wrong. With one week to go it was decided that we must try to get John Brimble on to the summit. This objective was in no way technically difficult, yet for John it was a major physical test.

John Brimble suffers from asthma, so much so that he is registered disabled because of it. Usually this presents no great problem as he takes a variety of inhalers and medication. Therein lay the snag. After the descent from Jostedalsbreen someone had mislaid John's medication, spares and all. They now lay on some minor northern road, of no use to John at all. Despite this lack of medical security John insisted on making an attempt on the summit. This we set out to do the following morning.

Mick, John Brimble and I packed our pulk in the early morning sun of a glorious day. Everyone else stayed in camp to carry out urgent repairs to kit. It would be their turn the following day.

In reality the climb up in to the summit plateau is no more than a snow plod; a long snow plod, yet no more. As we set off, the whole surrounding area of Norway unfolded below us like a great giant map. Gone was the mist, leaving in its place a stunning array of fjords and peaks, ice and snow.

With this majestic backdrop behind him John Brimble moved slowly up the hill. He was bent double. Leaning on one small ice-axe he towed the laden pulk behind him. Not content with just being a passenger, he wanted to carry the day's food and spare kit. He walked, sometimes stumbling and sometimes falling. Ahead of him his two companions stopped. They were on skis and not subject to the difficulties of moving over soft snow. After a while he moved up level to them. He didn't speak, couldn't speak. Instead he just gazed out over the far distant horizon, a smile on his face. In a while he moved off, slowly but surely ever upwards.

Late that afternoon the three of us reached the summit plateau. John was tired yet not in obvious discomfort. We were above the clouds at a height of 1,644 metres. For anyone with healthy lungs it was nothing in terms of any great height. For someone with damaged lungs, without medication, it may as well have been Everest.

In recognition of John's achievement the gods were good to us. To the west sparkled the great fjords leading out into the sea. To the east lay the awesome Hardangervidda plateau. Below us in the south there lay mountain after mountain, unimpeded by anything else. North was Jostedalsbreen, not visible to the naked eye, yet it was there, silent and brooding.

We stayed a while on that plateau. Time stopped and nothing else really mattered. All three of us were equal, disability or no disability. For people are only viewed as disabled in the eyes of man. And at that moment we were not under the eyes of man. We were under the eyes of nature. Nature makes no such discrimination. Under her gaze we all enter life, live it and die, some of us sooner than others, but that is life. We all yield only to nature, not man.

It was time to go. All of a sudden the air temperature began to drop and there was a bite in the wind. The dragon was returning. With the wind in our hair and gravity on our side we speeded down the slope. In no time at all we were safely situated down on the valley floor with a hot brew on the go and our boots off. It wasn't until some time later that Mick informed me that all the way up John was coughing up blood. John had never said a word.

13

INTEGRATION OR SEGREGATION?

I have been a stranger in a strange land.
Exodus 18:iii

Coughing up blood, not being able to see, unable to walk or talk. None of these is a barrier to taking part in an expedition of any kind. As I write these words, a group is planning to take someone in a chair up a Himalayan peak. Another expedition is planning to take disabled people ballooning over Mount Kenya. And John Birdsall, an explorer from Milton Keynes, confined to an electric chair is planning to lead his own expedition to Iceland.

Personality is a barrier. It creates the same problems on a purely able-bodied, normal expedition as it does on an integrated expedition. It was a clash of personalities that raised the question in Norway as to whether we were indeed integrated or in fact segregated.

In the space of one hour we had moved a distance of approximately 100 metres. We were on flat ground, in sight of the ski hut and using cross-country skis. Ahead of us Mick and John Brimble had disappeared up the mountain, also on skis. John Brimble had never seen a pair of skis in his life before, never mind used them. I stood in despair, John Sanders had fallen over again. My patience was wearing thin. No, that is a lie, it had plain worn out. For one hour I had tried to get John to move over the snow on his skis. The day before he had been teaching John Brimble to ski. He even told us that every year for the past six years he had enjoyed a week's skiing in Scotland. Something was definitely amiss somewhere.

Finally, enough was enough, we left the slopes and headed back to wait for the others. While waiting, I tried to find out why John had carried on the way he had. The problem was not a lack of aptitude on the skis, nor was it a lack of will to climb the ice-cap. Try as I might I could not find a reason for John's behaviour. Since coming down from the ice-cap crossing John had steadily withdrawn into himself. All had tried their best to integrate him and help him. At times we did succeed, yet towards the end of the expedition our efforts were in vain.

Mick and John Brimble came back from the mountain and joined in our chat. It was a frank and honest talk as to what we had done wrong and how we might resolve our problem. After some time John Sanders admitted that he had manipulated the rest of the expedition members in order to get out of camp chores and jobs. Here was the crux of the problem. All the trips John had been on in the past had been geared to providing disabled people an experience of a lifetime. They had been purely an experience. On our trip we had expected John to pull his own weight. This, we had found out, was not what he expected. As a result, he had in some way rebelled when he was asked to wash pots, pack his gear or make tea. This was not a result of his disability. We could have had the same problem with an able-bodied member of the expedition. However, what it does highlight is that the disability has to be taken into consideration, and this aspect never has to be faced by a so-called normal expedition.

When Zelda and Paul drove up the valley in the early afternoon, they came upon a rather sombre group of people. What annoyed and saddened me most was that John Sanders had taken all our efforts and help for granted. As we climbed into the Land Rover I made my biggest leadership error of the expedition. I asked John to tell everyone what he had told us that afternoon. This was fatal. Paul couldn't believe it and openly attacked John for his behaviour. Even Zelda, who is one of the most patient and considerate people I have ever met, was disgusted. With a few days to go, the team was divided. As we drove down to camp not even the setting sun over the distant mountains could raise the spirits of six rather disillusioned people.

A roster was organized; a roster for a different person each day to spend the time with John in camp sorting out kit for the journey home. Paul lost one of our radios on the road up to the ice-cap and the weather clamped down. Our great ideals of integrating disabled people into a private expedition had vanished over the horizon just like the fine weather we had been enjoying.

The rest of our time in Norway passed by quickly despite our problems. After many meetings we had gone some way to resolving the black mood that had gripped the expedition. We spent the remaining days exploring the ice-cap above us. The good weather returned as if to symbolize the reconciliation in the team. Although not forgotten, the events of the past days were put to the back of our minds. On the final evening before we had to head back to Bergen, Zelda and I skied high up on to the ice-cap with the intention of sleeping out under the stars on the snow. It was to be the perfect end to a fast-concluding expedition.

Two inert bodies lay on an island of rock amidst a vast expanse of white ocean. Above them great clouds rolled over and beyond the mountains surrounding them. Behind them the moon shone, in front of them the sun sank below the fjords.

It was cold, clear and crisp. The problems we faced as a team and I as leader evaporated into the night. Up on the silent icy waste we were once again reminded of our mortality.

We awoke to the steady drizzle of rain and the damp clammy breath of mist. The dragon had returned. It was time to leave this country of natural wonder and head back home to face the music. In a spectacular English fashion we skied down over hard ice. In a tumble of limbs, skis and packs we fell of the ice-cap and into the Land Rover.

Within twenty-four hours we were sitting in the bar on the MS *Venus*, seasick pills at the ready and the beer to wash them down with. In no time at all the land of rock and ice, fjords and mountains was fast sinking over the horizon and into the wake of the ship as it steadily ploughed its way to Blighty. Already it was all just a memory.

14

A LESSON LEARNT AND AN ADVENTURE IN THE OFFING

If you can fill the unforgiving minute
With sixty seconds' worth of distance run,
Yours is the Earth and everything that's in it.
Kipling

And so it ended. It wasn't a great expedition in any stretch of the word. Yet, I hope we tried to achieve an ideal; an ideal to integrate and involve disabled people in a realm of life that has been exclusively the domain of able-bodied people.

Crossing the North Sea was uneventful thankfully. As we approached England only then did the beauty of the land we had left hit us. Norway had been clear and fresh, its coastline well defined and bold. In stark contrast the coast of England was dull and insignificant. It was a depressing sight.

Like a bat out of hell Mick drove us home. We all had jobs to resume. For me the spectre of what to tell people was looming fast. I had a duty to report on the expedition, yet, what did I tell? If I told the 'true, no holds barred' story our trip would look a sham. Yes, we had crossed the ice-cap, but had we compromised our main aim of integration to do so? What would John Sanders tell his parents? A whirl of questions ran amok as we hurtled along a congested A1.

John Sanders was dropped off at home first. His mother was not amused and the atmosphere very hostile as a result of John's initial comments. We left in haste. Not a word of thank-you, just a goodbye. Mick had enjoyed the experience, I think, and wanted to go back. Paul has since said he won't go on a trip with me again, for reasons I have yet to ascertain. Zelda loved it, despite everything, and John Brimble? John Brimble came up to me just before we left Bergen. It was early morning and the sun was dancing off the fjord. 'It's been the best time of my life, thank-you.' We had achieved our aim.

Real life hit like a hammer blow. Within a day of returning from Norway all our equipment had to be returned. I opened nine grim letters from the bank and headed off at six o'clock the next morning to work in a factory. Ice-caps and fjords could not be further away.

A period of nervous waiting followed my immediate return from the expedition. Nervous in terms of what John Sanders would say to his mother. Yet my fears were unfounded. Although John was unhappy with his expedition I'm sure he learnt a lot from the experience. As a leader I learnt an immense amount, mainly in terms of general expedition leadership. In terms of disabled and integrated expeditions the iceberg was just starting to show.

I believe that we did our level best in Norway to integrate everyone in the framework of the trip. It may be true that we failed with John Sanders, however, this was not due to his disability but a result of his personality. It was also a result of the interaction between John and the rest of the team and the way I as leader dealt with the situation as it developed. Taking someone into an environment such as Jostedalsbreen is a risk. The risk is doubled when a portion of your team is disabled, in whatever capacity. To combat this, one has to make sure the planning is meticulous and nothing is left to chance. Saying this, I accept that a great deal of our success was due to Lady Luck and the grace of her touch. However, I dare to say that most expedition firsts and daring trips are due to a large amount of luck. Yet glowing letters from Ranulph Fiennes, and the reception I received after many slide shows indicated that we did at least do a lot right.

Six months on from Norway and the expedition is now a memory. A memory that has been passed on to many different interested groups, not least the Royal Geographical Society. Every year the RGS holds an expedition seminar geared towards undergraduate expeditions. As a direct result of my Norway trip I was asked to chair a workshop on disabled expeditions. In between lofty talks on polar, mountaineering and desert trips, a small gathering of people met in the tearoom. It was a pioneering meeting concluding with a passionate desire for the RGS to hold a full seminar on all aspects of disabled expeditions. Later on, after several glasses of rather nice red wine, I approached Nigel Winser, a prominent figure at the Society. 'Put something on paper and send it me. If you're prepared to put your head on the chopping block and organize it, do it.' Nigel Winser's words cut through the wine and smoke. The floodgate to greater awareness in terms of disabled expeditions was beginning to open.

Perhaps one day we will see disabled people walk to the South Pole, the North Pole, cross Greenland and climb the world's highest peaks. With courage and vision all these are possible. People such as Norman Croucher and Jack Vander Molen have shown us the way; it is up to us to follow.

For me Norway was a stepping-stone, with a little luck in 1996 a small team integrating disabled people will parachute on to the Greenland ice-cap traversing the ice-cap along the Arctic Circle. A pioneering journey following in the footsteps of explorers such as Watkins and Croft it should raise a greater interest in disabled trips. Plans are now well afoot for the first 'Disabled Explorer' expedition seminar. Such a seminar will surely increase awareness, not only amongst the public in general, but also the exploration fraternity at large.

Unfortunately, as I write these words, my time at Fountaindale is drawing to a close; life will never be the same again. Government cutbacks, politics and economic considerations take no heed of individual child needs or of caring staff.

A lone Union Flag flutters in the wind. It is surrounded by snowcapped fairy tale mountains. Standing by the flag are four people, dressed in a manner suitable to the remote situation they are in. By their feet are three white a red fibreglass sledges containing their precious equipment. There is no sound, just the flapping of a flag in the evening breeze. It could have been a scene anywhere in the world. Antarctica, Greenland, Siberia or even Patagonia. Yet one of the group cannot see the peaks around him. Blind since the age of two he has travelled across the icy waste of Europe's highest ice-cap. Blind in sight but not blind in vision, yet it is not sight that takes one to the great spaces of the world. It is vision. Vision took Ran Fiennes across Antarctica. Vision will take disabled people to the wide open country.

Four people move off down the glacier. The Union Flag put away, they move slowly down the frozen river of ice. Ahead of them the sun begins to set; setting over the mountains but not over the new horizon of integrated expeditions.

A battered Union Flag, flown proudly on the Jostedalsbreen ice-cap now hangs on a wall at Fountaindale School. Waiting.

APPENDIX I

SPECIALIST CONSIDERATIONS FOR INTEGRATED AND DISABLED EXPEDITIONS

In the next few pages I have endeavoured to put down some useful information which might help in planning an integrated expedition. It is by no means definitive, only a guide. For more detailed advice and information there is a list of useful contacts.

Clearly an expedition which aims to involve disabled people is somewhat different from a purely able-bodied one. This section aims to highlight these considerations using this expedition as a model.

Disabled trips take two forms: there are those which aim to provide an experience for disabled people, for example, by taking them to the beach to enjoy and experience the sea. In this case there is no integration as the group is purely providing support for a group of disabled people. The second form of trip is somewhat different. It will aim to involve the disabled person as much as possible in a project not specifically geared towards disabled people. This kind of trip then becomes a fully integrated trip where both parties work towards a common goal. It is important when considering involving disabled people to bear this in mind. Do you just want to provide an experience for someone who is blind or do you want them to work alongside able-bodied people as an equal? At present the greater majority of expeditions and outdoor pursuits for the disabled only provide an experience.

Our trip set out to integrate disabled people with able-bodied people, working towards a common goal in an extreme and dangerous environment.

The nature of the disability may be a limiting factor. The vast range of disabilities is mind-blowing. Essentially in terms of expeditions you need to consider whether the person is wheelchair-bound, electric chair-bound or walking.

It is important that a clear goal is established and the team members are capable of achieving this. Our first and foremost aim was integration in a private trip. One cannot do this, however, unless a real goal is set. Our initial goal was to take a wheelchair user across the highest glacier system in Europe. Paramount to a safe expedition is a reconnaissance trip if possible, training weekends and bags of research. As a result of these activities we had to alter our plans and consider the following: general camping arrangements, toileting drills, medical requirements and transport arrangements.

When camping with someone with a disability you may need to allow twice the normal time required to make and break camp. At least two to three people need to be allocated as carers, if needed to provide twenty-four hour care. This of course can put a greater demand on all team members. Our team was lucky in that everyone helped out and provided constant professional attention to the needs of its disabled members.

Medication required will depend on the nature of the disability. However, doctors' letters are vital to ensure that the person is fit to undertake the expedition or at the very least a reference from a close relative. This raises the question as to whether or not a medically qualified person is needed on the team. In our case we decided against this, simply because of the fact that had there been an accident on the ice-cap, all a doctor would have been able to do was provide a diagnosis and first aid. This was what we could have provided anyway if someone had been hurt. Anything major would require an immediate evacuation to the nearest hospital anyway. Of course this all depends on the area you are in. I would suggest that anywhere more remote and it would be advisable to have someone with some form of medical training.

In terms of taking someone in a wheelchair on to an ice-cap or indeed a mountain, there are extra problems. The most daunting is, of course, how do you get them up the hill? There is only one way — by stretcher. If you have unlimited cash you could in theory hire a helicopter. However, such an option is only open to very few expeditions. Carrying a stretcher uphill is extremely tiring. With a disabled person on it you will need not only four people at each end but also one on each side to stabilize the person. Expedition members need to be selected so that they can fulfil this physically demanding task.

Once on the snow or ice there as yet appears to be no specific sledge system designed for wheelchair-bound people to propel themselves across flat snow. An adapted sit ski is the best option at the moment. Are there any other items of special equipment you may need? For example, hoists for people with brittle bones, inhalers for asthma sufferers, nappies and bedpans for toileting or even spare chair batteries and tyres. The bottom line is whoever you take, check thoroughly that you have covered everything. This will need to be done by talking to the person's doctor, carer, parents and school or college.

Frostbite and hypothermia risk is greatly increased in someone confined to a chair. This is as a result of decreased circulation in the lower body and an inability to move, of course. When you're nice and warm they may be suffering severe frostbite, yet they won't even know about it, due to the lack of any sensation in the lower body.

However, we took a registered blind person across the ice-cap and someone with severe lung problems on to the summit of another. It is a useful point to know that being registered fully blind is a legal classification, not a medical one. At all times in mountain terrain a carer was allocated. A safe number for taking a blind person is a ratio of three to one. To take one person in a chair into the same situation you may need six to one; four to constantly look after the disabled person and two to concentrate on camp chores etc. We also employed tent rosters to relieve the pressure of caring all the time.

In spite of all the problems I believe it is essential that disabled people be treated as 'normal'. This belief is born out of teaching PE to severely disabled children. The last thing they want to be treated as is disabled. One has only to make allowances in certain areas. At Fountaindale we still manage to teach gym, games, dance, outdoor education and swimming. Everyone is disabled in one way or another, be it an inability to see or not being able to read French. This expedition set out to treat its disabled members as normally as possible. It is perhaps important to bear in mind that people who have been born with a disability have a different approach to those who have become disabled. In my experience people born disabled are sometimes overly protected and are more demanding. On the other hand those disabled as a result of an accident are more outgoing, they may not even view themselves as disabled.

My ideas and philosophy may be viewed as harsh by some, yet it is the only way disabled people will achieve full integration into the expedition framework.

It is desirable but not essential that you have someone with experience of disabled people on the trip. Zelda and I have had a wide range of experience with both children and adults.

We expected the disabled members on the trip to participate fully in all areas of the expedition. In one case this happened, in the other it did not. This was not because the person concerned was not capable, it was simply because on previous trips he had not been expected to. However, with regular meetings such problems can be resolved. It is vital that at the start of the trip the disabled members are aware of their role and expectations, as is any other member.

The best advice is just to go and do it, for as Shackleton said, 'difficulties are just problems to be overcome'.

If you want a fully integrated expedition then you need to treat the disabled as you would anyone else. I believe you should set an objective and then decide how to achieve it, not pick some disabled people and gear the objective to them. They should be geared towards the objective. Only then will the expedition become integrated as all members will work towards the common aim.

The above is only a basic guide. For more information refer to the suggested reading list and the contacts given. If they don't know they'll know a man who can.

APPENDIX II

USEFUL ADDRESSES

The following may be useful in either providing expert advice, specific information or guidance:

Calvert Trust, Keilder Water, Hexham, Northumberland, NE48 1BS
Tel: 01434 250232
Churchtown Farm Field Studies Centre, Lanlivery, Bodmin, Cornwall Tel: 01208 872148
Lifequest, 11 Churchill Park, Colwick, Nottingham, NG4 2HF
Fieldfare Trust, 67a The Wicker, Sheffield, S3 8HT
Tel: 0114 2701668
Fountaindale School, Nottingham Road, Mansfield, Notts. NG18 5BA Tel: 01623 792671
MacIntyre Adventure, Thames Regional Office, 26 Darin Court, Crownhill, Milton Keynes, MK8 0BE Tel: 01908 262056
Oxventure, 28 Beech Road, Wheatley, Oxford, OX9 1UR
The British Paralympic Association, Delta Point, Room G13A, 35 Wellesley Road, Croydon, Surrey, CR9 2YZ
Tel: 0181 666 4556
The British Sports Association for the Disabled, Solecast House, 13–27 Brunswick Place, London, N1 6DX Tel: 0171 490 4919
The Paul Vander Molen Foundation, The Model Farm House, Church End, Hendon, London, NW4 4JS Tel: 0171 1214/2344
The Royal Geographical Society, 1 Kensington Gore, London, SW7
Tim Reddish, Disabled Sports Development Officer, 24 Nuthall Gardens, Western Boulevard, Nottingham

United Kingdom Sports Association for People with Mental Handicap, 30 Philip Lane, Tottenham, London, N15 4JB Tel: 0181 855 1177

Uphill Ski Club of Great Britain, c/o The Spastics Society (SCOPE), 12 Park Crescent, London, W1N 4EQ Tel: 0171 636 1989

BIBLIOGRAPHY

Fiennes, Ranulph, *Icefall In Norway*, 1972, Hodder & Stoughton Ltd., London

Fiennes, Ranulph, *Mind Over Matter*, 1993, Sinclair-Stevenson, London

Hawkridge, John, *Uphill All The Way*, 1991, Michael Joseph Ltd., London

Lennon, Peter, *Scandinavian Mountains*, 1987, West Col, Reading

Winser, Shane & McWilliam, Nicholas, *Expedition Planners Handbook & Directory 1993–94*, 1992, Edpedition Advisory Centre, London

Then they all went home again.

And I think, but am not quite sure, that Roo had a hot bath

and went straight to bed. But Pooh went back to his own house,

and feeling very proud of what he had done,

had a little something to revive himself.

A. A. Milne, 1926